Aliens and Christianity: Threat or Vindication?

Aidan Ashby

Publisher: The Good Report

thegoodreport.co.uk

ISBN: 9798851489358

CONTENTS

PROLOGUE

Imagine the scenario.

On an otherwise ordinary spring morning, a cloud of 200 shimmering silver shapes plummets through Earth's atmosphere at 10,000 mph. Each object is 20–80 feet long, with various forms such as ovals, cubes, and tic-tacs. None of them have wings or exhaust plumes, and none of them originate from Earth. The crafts split up and head to different capital cities across the globe. Beams of light flare from the bottom of each craft, scanning the terrain, while the air around them buzzes gently. After zigzagging erratically like ice hockey pucks, each silver shape eventually comes to rest three feet above the ground in front of the senate, parliament, or palace of every earthly nation.

Every TV channel and radio station is interrupted by an emergency broadcast, and the world holds its breath.

A being steps forth. The aliens have finally landed.

What would this do to your worldview? Which of your strongly held beliefs would be shaken, and what would remain unchanged?

Everyone has an opinion on aliens. If any of us ever saw something extraordinary in the sky, we would inevitably jump to whatever conclusion most easily conformed to our existing worldview. A naturalist might expect it to be some kind of foreign military tech. A

Christian, Jew, or Muslim might look up and see an angel. A sci-fi fan would probably have biological aliens from outer space in mind. We all jump to conclusions like this, and it makes sense – we take cognitive shortcuts to quickly integrate new information with our existing picture of the world.

This is a topic that stretches credulity. Is it really worth investing all that time and electricity to write and read about aliens, something so bizarre and little known? It brings to mind the famous and derided question, "How many angels can dance on the head of a pin?" that legend says scholastic theologians debated within the walls of Constantinople while Turkish invaders approached the city.

But while science occasionally forces a shift in the Western religious worldview to accommodate new discoveries, science often finds itself playing catch-up. In his book God and the Astronomers, Robert Jastrow describes how the discovery of evidence for the Big Bang constituted a wake-up call for naturalism:

"For the scientist who has lived by his faith in the power of reason, the story ends like a bad dream. He has scaled the mountains of ignorance; he is about to conquer the highest peak; as he pulls himself over the final rock, he is greeted by a band of theologians who have been sitting there for centuries."[1]

The purpose of this book is not to convince you that aliens exist (and in fact, I'll make a case against the existence of some forms of alien life). You may be a

---

[1] Jastrow, 1981

believer, a sceptic or just slightly bemused to have found this book. But the thing is, the idea of alien life challenges some really important areas of every major modern worldview. The idea of the existence of aliens presses on the core of our identity as humans, it challenges our place in the universe, and, for Christians, it questions the nature of our God-given purpose. So, we will use this as a powerful hypothetical scenario to explore what impact proof of the existence of alien life would have on the Christian faith. Using a range of hypotheses we'll see just how far we can push the boundaries to find the theological red lines for Christianity.

This book may also be helpful for anyone who is wrestling through their Christian faith in light of UFOlogy.

PART 1:

ALIEN IMAGING, INCARNATION AND REDEMPTION

1. THE PROBLEM

Most people believe that the discovery of alien life would destroy most of the major world religions, and it's easy to see why. From beginning to end, the biblical story revolves around the relationship between heaven and earth. While Hebraic scripture describes three realms of heaven (earth's sky, the celestial realm of planets and stars, and the home realm of God), "heaven and earth" is set up as a dichotomy, a pairing as natural as male and female. The relationship between heaven and earth is used as a metaphor for the relationship between God and His creation. The Bible's geo- and anthropocentrism is striking.

The story begins with the creation of heaven and earth, with earth established as God's temple, the location of His throne in this universe, and the Edenic location of His divine council. Humanity serves as His mediator, His primary representatives enacting His rule in nature.

Although our story is riddled with sin and rebellion against God, there remains something unique and important about humanity among all created beings. This rebellion propelled God to take on human flesh for humanity's redemption. The God-man dies, and His resurrection draws all believing humanity with Him into a new creation order.

The story concludes with the revealing and glorification of the human sons of God. The rest of creation is then drawn into this renewal. The story ends with the marriage of a new heaven and earth, with God dwelling permanently with humanity, in a human city.

That's the story. It's not just that the story only recounts the action that happens on earth; but that the most cosmically significant action occurs on earth.

Overcoming bad arguments first

Sometimes, Christians propose a somewhat flawed argument against the existence of extraterrestrial life, suggesting that if such beings existed, the Bible would have certainly mentioned them, so they probably don't exist. However, this reasoning is weak as it relies on an argument from silence, a logical fallacy that assumes the absence of explicit mention indicates non-existence. However, the Bible doesn't mention kangaroos, yet we know they exist. The scale of consideration may be different, but the underlying principle is the same.

Diving deeper, one might question how we could be certain about what God would or wouldn't reveal to us. It's entirely plausible that He had compelling reasons to not mention extraterrestrials in the scriptures, if they indeed exist. An example could be the possibility of humans becoming overly fixated on alien beings. This fascination could lead to a misplaced hope of salvation from these creatures, gravely overshadowing our essential relationship with God.

Alternatively, one might consider that God may not have deemed it necessary to inform us about the existence of extraterrestrials. Scripture does not provide explicit details on the origin of angels or the existence of galaxies.

This parallels the lack of direct mention of heliocentrism – the scientific understanding that Earth and its neighbouring planets orbit the sun.

Applying the same "He would have told us" logic could potentially negate heliocentrism. Intriguingly, geocentrism proponents, although misguided, could cite more biblical texts supporting their misguided stance than there are scriptures discrediting the existence of aliens. However, biblical scholars generally agree that the writers of ancient scripture wrote within the understanding of their contemporary geocentric cosmology, not to impart scientific knowledge, but to communicate theological truths.

In contemporary times, we have seamlessly integrated a scientifically validated heliocentric cosmology into our theology. As believers in God as the creator of the heavens and earth, we assert that God designed the system in which Earth revolves around the sun. This belief stands even though scripture more frequently writes within a geocentric model. But the core truth remains the same – God is the creator and sustainer of all things.

This highlights that theological understanding can and has evolved to incorporate scientific discovery without diminishing the foundational belief system. Such flexibility might pave the way for the integration of potential discoveries, like extraterrestrial life, into our theological frameworks. But I'll let you in on a little secret. The crux of the matter isn't really about the existence of aliens; it's actually all about humanity and Christology – the person, nature, and role of Christ.

I'm going to explore this by assessing several scenarios – what would be the consequences if there existed alien pets, our near-peers, or phantoms? What would happen if they were more like critters, cousins, or cosmic spirits? In part one, I'll address the first two scenarios, with the third option left for part two.

2. THE DISCOVERY OF ALIEN PETS

We'll begin with the simpler scenario – aliens as pets. In this situation, NASA sends a submarine rover to Saturn's icy volcanic moon Europa, and it discovers blue prokaryotic slime clustered around an underwater volcanic vent. Alternatively, this pet could be as intelligent as a dog (let's make it a flying dog named Pluto, just for fun) but not as intelligent as a human.

How likely?

Numerous theories have attempted to calculate the probability of the existence of biological alien life and to explain why we haven't discovered it yet. The most famous of these is the Fermi paradox, which inspired the Drake equation.

In the summer of 1950, four physicists were walking to lunch, discussing recent UFO reports and the possibility of faster-than-light travel. The conversation shifted to other topics, but during lunch, Enrico Fermi blurted out, "But where is everybody?"[2]

Named after Fermi's question, the Fermi Paradox has since been expanded into the following line of reasoning:

1.   There are billions of stars in the Milky Way similar

---

[2] Jones, 1985

to the Sun.

2. With high probability, some of these stars have Earth-like planets in a circumstellar habitable zone.

3. Many of these stars, and hence their planets, are much older than the Sun. If the Earth is typical, some may have developed intelligent life long ago.

4. Some of these civilisations may have developed interstellar travel, a step humans are investigating now.

5. Even at the slow pace of currently envisioned interstellar travel, the Milky Way galaxy could be completely traversed in a few million years.

6. And since many of the stars similar to the Sun are billions of years older, Earth should have already been visited by extraterrestrial civilisations, or at least their probes.

7. However, there is no convincing evidence that this has happened.

Surely, the cosmos is so vast that someone should have reached out to us by now? Wouldn't it be the height of arrogance to think that humanity is the most intelligent form of life to exist in this boundless universe? It seems intuitively correct, but these intuitions mask some significant assumptions.

Turning this basic theory into an equation, astrophysicist Frank Drake presented the Drake equation in 1961, which aimed to determine the number (N) of technically advanced civilisations in the Milky Way Galaxy, taking into account astronomical, biological, and psychological factors.

In simplified form, the logic of his equation seeks to

determine:

1. The rate of star formation in our galaxy
2. What fraction of those stars develop planetary systems
3. What fraction of those planets would be ecologically suitable for life to form
4. What fraction of those habitable planets would life actually begin on
5. What fraction of those life forms would evolve intelligence
6. What fraction of those intelligent life forms would invent technology at least capable of interstellar communication
7. Finally, the average lifetime of such advanced civilisations

The primary issue with this equation is that all the numbers are poorly known, and the uncertainty increases progressively with each factor in the equation. This leads to vastly different predictions, depending on the numbers you input. One 2020 study[3] that analysed data from the Kepler spacecraft calculated that our galaxy could be home to as many as six billion Earth-like planets, while another study by the SETI Institute[4] estimated the number at around 300 million. That's a 20-fold difference. As Encyclopedia Britannica further explains:

> *"...if civilizations characteristically destroy themselves within a decade of achieving radio astronomy, which is taken as a marker of an advanced civilization, then $N = 1$, and there*

---

[3] Kunimoto & Matthews, 2020
[4] SETI Institute, 2020

are no other intelligent life forms in the Galaxy with whom terrestrial researchers can communicate. If, on the other hand, it is assumed that one percent of the civilizations learn to live with the technology of mass destruction and themselves, then N = 1,000,000, and the nearest advanced civilization would be on average a few hundred light-years away."[5]

Since Drake's equation involves a series of estimations with accumulating uncertainties, it fails to provide any practical clarity regarding the likelihood of biological alien life of any kind in our galaxy. As Michael Crichton, MD and anthropologist, explains:

"This serious-looking equation gave SETI [the Search for ExtraTerrestrial Intelligence institute] a serious footing as a legitimate intellectual inquiry. The problem, of course, is that none of the terms can be known, and most cannot even be estimated. The only way to work the equation is to fill in with guesses. And guesses—just so we're clear—are merely expressions of prejudice. Nor can there be 'informed guesses.' If you need to state how many planets with life choose to communicate, there is simply no way to make an informed guess. It is simply prejudice."[6]

We can extend our argument even further. It's not just that we can't know the likelihood of finding biological life; we can, in fact, safely conclude that alien life is highly improbable unless it has been specially created by an intelligence. This relates to the fourth factor of Drake's equation: the likelihood of life emerging on a planet.

---

[5] Drake Equation | Astronomy | Britannica, 2023
[6] Crichton, 2008, from a lecture delivered by Chrichton at MIT on Jan. 17, 2003

As the universe is incredibly vast, intuition naturally leads one to think there's ample opportunity for life to emerge. Yet all these optimistic predictions for the abundance of biological ET (extraterrestrial) life seem to completely overlook the astonishingly low probability of life accidentally developing from non-living matter anywhere, including on Earth.

The evolutionary processes of mutation and natural selection aren't enough for abiogenesis, as these processes require some kind of pre-existing prebiotic system with its own genetic code that can then mutate to produce new traits that can be selected for. Moreover, any viable prebiotic structure would need to have entire ecosystems of parts working together by chance before that system could endure long enough, all arising from non-living matter. Furthermore, this mutating machinery is as complex as a sprawling factory, with each component constructed of intricate arrangements of proteins. These proteins themselves are complex entities that would have to form by chance from amino acids. For a detailed breakdown of the probability of a single useful protein forming by chance, see this 9-minute video[7].

Researchers have calculated that on ancient Earth, the probability of a single, smaller-than-average functional protein forming by chance was 1 in 10^{164}. And that only gives you one protein. The simplest living cell we know of contains over 300 different proteins, but proteins are only part of the puzzle. DNA, RNA, lipids, and a host of other molecules also play vital roles in the intricate ballet of life. Sure, biological life could be built out of something other than proteins, but due to how well-suited proteins are to

[7] Illustra Media, 2016

the job, that's even less likely.

The complexity and specificity of life suggest that its emergence isn't a mere roll of cosmic dice. These immense odds underscore the profound mystery of life's origins, a mystery that continues to captivate our curiosity.

All this makes the genesis of biological life by chance alone extraordinarily unlikely. With that considered, the likelihood of biological life emerging independently a second time in the universe, wholly unconnected to Earth, would be even less likely to have occurred by chance. Therefore, the existence of alien biological life would only strengthen the case for an intelligent non-biological designer[8] operating in the universe. They would more likely be another special direct creation of God or the overlords of our simulation, whatever you want to call it. Nonetheless, I'd require an exceptionally compelling reason to believe that such entities - be they living blue slimes or flying dogs – truly originated from outside Earth.

But why not?

Some people ask why God wouldn't create more life. Why did God make the universe so vast, and why the incredible waste?

This objection often comes from theists who want to believe in aliens. It's certainly an appealing idea - perhaps one day we will all dance around in heaven with myriads of angels and a colourful panoply of aliens from across the universe.

However, the thing is, this vast universe is not a waste to God, as if He has only a limited supply of stardust. The

---

[8] Frankowski, 2008

universe isn't big to God, and 100 billion years isn't a long time. He metaphorically holds the universe in the palm of His hand (Isaiah 40:12) and a thousand years pass like a few hours to Him (Psalm 90:4). As Psalm 19 says, the heavens declare the glory of God.

So why did God make the universe so vast? Perhaps He wished to pour out one drop of His grandeur by creating almost innumerable stars, planets, quasars, galaxies, superclusters, and so on. No extravagance is wasteful to a being of infinite power and resources.

Returning to the 'alien pet' scenario: we have some blue slime or a flying dog. These newly discovered creatures would serve the same purpose as all the plants and animals that live on Earth: they would exist to exalt and honour God, reflecting His magnificence through their own splendour.

And just like all nonhuman life on Earth, these alien "pets" wouldn't need saving from their sins. With the rest of creation, they would "wait in eager expectation for the [human] children of God to be revealed… in hope that the creation itself will be liberated from its bondage to decay and brought into the freedom and glory of the children of God" (Romans 8:19-22)

In the wake of such a discovery the scientific community would start to grapple with the far-reaching implications and the field of astrobiology would undoubtedly see a significant surge in funding and interest. However, from the perspective of Christian theology, little would have to change. The overarching narrative would remain: all creation, terrestrial or otherwise, exists to glorify the Creator, and human salvation continues to be central to God's divine plan. The revelation of life beyond

Earth, then, becomes another testament to the infinite power and magnificence of God.

3. MEETING OUR ALIEN PEERS

Now, by "alien peers," I'm referring to intelligent biological aliens. We are their closest equals on Earth. Perhaps they're vastly more intelligent than us, with technology that would make Elon Musk envious, but they're fundamentally biological like us. They may see us as equals or as mere ants to be studied, but we're the ones they'd seek out first if they were ever interested in communicating with Earth life. Originating from a physical place within our shared spacetime continuum, they too navigate three spatial dimensions and one temporal dimension.

Now, if the low probability of chance abiogenesis would make the discovery of "alien pets" another sign of God's special creation, then finding an extremely intelligent alien biological peer would only raise the stakes. This scenario is the most challenging of the three and, in my opinion, the least likely to turn out to be the case.

But the real challenge of this scenario lies elsewhere. Discovering alien peers would raise issues in three areas of Christian theology, all related to creation:

1. **Imaging:** What does it mean to be made in the image of God? Are these aliens also the image of God, and does that threaten our status as the image of God?

2. **Incarnation:** Did God ever incarnate as an alien

in the same way He took on human flesh? Is there
an alien Jesus?

3. **Redemption:** Can aliens be redeemed? Did Jesus
die for our alien peers too? What place would they
have in the new creation?

These three core tenets of the Christian faith are where
the rubber hits the road.

Aliens as the image of God

Would the existence of intelligent aliens challenge the
idea that humanity is the image of God? To answer this,
we must ask what it means to be the image and likeness of
God.

*"Then God said, 'Let us make mankind in our image, in
our likeness, so that they may rule over the fish in the sea and
the birds in the sky, over the livestock and all the wild
animals, and over all the creatures that move along the
ground.'*

*So God created mankind in his own image,
in the image of God he created them;
male and female he created them.*

*God blessed them and said to them, 'Be fruitful and increase
in number; fill the earth and subdue it. Rule over the fish in
the sea and the birds in the sky and over every living creature
that moves on the ground.'"*
- Genesis 1:26-28

Whatever the image of God is, Christian orthodoxy
considers it inherent to what it means to be human. It is

15

typically understood that:

1. Because God made our ancestors in His image, every human descendant of those progenitors also inherited that image.
2. There are no degrees in the image. You either are the image of God or you are not.
3. While the expression of the image may be marred or forgotten, it cannot be lost or removed - it's "baked in" to our nature.

The Creation of Adam, by Michelangelo, compared to a human brain

When Michelangelo painted The Creation of Adam on the ceiling of the Sistine Chapel, he included some hidden symbolism. In the painting, as God reaches out to deliver the divine spark of life to the limp Adam, God forms the shape of a human brain, along with His shroud and entourage. According to Johns Hopkins professor and medical illustrator Ian Suk, this conforms "in very uncanny ways to the exact anatomical shape"[9] of a brain.

The message seems to be that consciousness or rationality is the true gift a creator can give to its creation.

So, what does it mean to be the image of God? The prevailing view is that it signifies we are like God in that we share particular traits in our psychological or spiritual

---

[9] Becker, 2016

makeup – this is known as the substantive view. Similarly, a self-portrait is an image of its maker – through its appearance, not through what it does. The unique traits often identified with this view include our rationality, moral conscience, sometimes our ability to speak, and finally, that we each have a living spirit capable of having a relationship with God.

The major problem with the substantive view is that we all have different capacities. If you defend the idea that being the image of God means we have superior intelligence, free choice, conscience, or whatever, then you must abandon any pro-life stance. How rational is a fetus? Is a psychopath made in the image of God, or is it as moral to kill them as any animal?

To state that we are the image of God because of our capabilities would require believing that we can possess the image of God in varying degrees and that losing our capacity would entail a diminishing of our image-bearing nature.

There are various abhorrent ideologies that have turned to the substantive view for support. Voltaire, the great humanist, cynic, and prominent critic of Christianity during the Enlightenment, wrote, *"it is a serious question among them whether the Africans are descended from monkeys or whether the monkeys come from them. Our wise men have said that man was created in the image of God. Now here is a lovely image of the Divine Maker: a flat and black nose with little or hardly any intelligence."*[10] Then in a 1923 speech in Munich, Hitler told the crowd, *"the Jew is certainly a race, but not human. He cannot be human in the sense of the image of God, of the Eternal. The Jew is the image of the devil."*[11]

---

[10] Aderibigbe, 2015, quoting Voltaire in Les Lettres d' Ameb, 1769

A second view, which I'll only briefly touch on as it's not held by many, is the idea that the image refers to our actual relationship with God, not just our capacity for relationship – the relational view. One problem with this view is that locating the image outside a human's inherent nature jeopardises it. People living in rebellion against God effectively sever their relationship with Him, which would contravene the idea that the image can't truly be lost.

However, the view held by most modern Old Testament/Hebrew Bible scholars is the functional view. This interprets the image of God as a vocation, a role that humans have in the created order in which God calls humankind to rule like Him as kings over the earth. Through comparative Ancient Near Eastern studies, scholars have discovered many ancient texts in which certain kings are exalted as the "images" of their respective deities, giving them a divine mandate to rule. Genesis 1 takes this common pattern but broadens it to all humanity, who are therefore called to reflect God's image by ruling life on earth according to the pattern of God who rules the entire universe.

As J. Richard Middleton described: "the imago Dei designates the royal office or calling of human beings as God's representatives or agents in the world."[12] As well as being a royal image, the functional view also entails a priestly role as humanity is called to represent God to the creation and to represent creation before God.

In my view, the functional perspective makes more sense of the immediate scriptural context of Genesis 1. When God declares His intention to make humanity as His

---

[11] Weikart, 2016
[12] Middleton, 1994, 27

image, He explicitly states the reason: "so that they may rule [over creation]." Then, right after carrying this out, He blesses them and commissions them to fill, subdue, and rule over the earth. Hence, being God's image is synonymous with acting as God's ruling representative – it's a vocation.

In the functional view, the image of God is located more in God's intentions for humanity than in our abilities, making it a more stable foundation for moral imperatives. Being vocational in nature, this view is also much more action-oriented; it doesn't just cause us to navel-gaze, admiring how wonderful and unique we are in all creation; instead, it points us outward toward our responsibility to act justly like God in the world, subduing chaos by ordering and caring for creation.

Of course, God has endowed humanity with certain abilities to help us fulfil our vocation. However, the functional view is not challenged by people's lack of capacity (e.g., physical or mental disability) or disinterest in a relationship with God, because the calling remains whatever our capacity or attitude toward God. In this view, it's also easier to justify why it's wrong to murder people (Genesis 9:5-6): to murder an official representative of God is to insult God Himself (Matthew 21:33-46). Hence, one of the main ways God calls us to express our love for Him is by loving our neighbour.

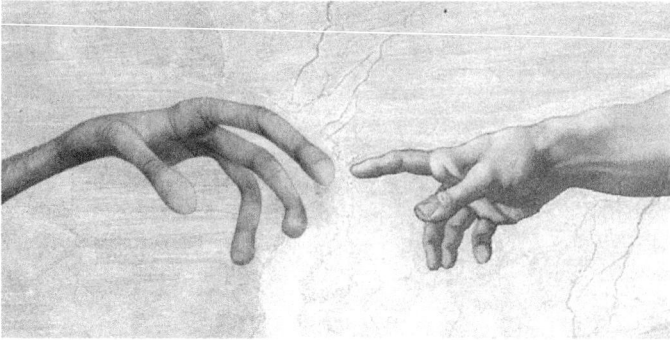

So, what does all this have to do with aliens?

Most people hold to a substantive view of the image of God and understand that our capabilities are what give us a unique status in creation. So, if we were to find aliens that were far more intelligent than us, that would challenge this view. Just as the existence of people with lesser capabilities would cause "an imaging problem" under the substantive view, these aliens would pose the opposite problem – they would represent more of the image of God than we do.

Of course, realising that we are no longer at the top of the intellectual food chain may not be such a bad thing for us: a little humility would do our species some good. Being overly concerned about being at the centre of everything is the sin of pride; it's what caused all this mess in the first place. In the biblical story of Job, God answers his complaints by giving him a safari tour of the created world, of the earth, of weather, of some magnificent creatures we do know and some astonishing creatures we don't. The point, God clarifies, is that Job is like dust compared to God. Although Job is made in the image of God, Job is not the centre of the universe. And neither are we.

But would the appearance of creatures who are more

the image of God than us automatically give them authority over us?

Fortunately, the functional view circumvents these issues. While our capacities help our vocation, they don't determine it. Humanity would still be God's chosen kings and queens on earth, no matter how many sublimely superior species crossed our paths.

And just in case this wasn't watertight enough, even if God had commissioned an intelligent alien species to act as His image somewhere else, that wouldn't necessarily unseat us. We're not the image of God because we're unique; we're unique on earth because we're the image of God, and nothing else on earth is. So being the image of God doesn't have to be a competitive affair. They would image God in their world, as we do in ours.

The friar and philosopher Thomas Aquinas considered the possibility of the existence of non-human yet highly rational creatures, and the potential impact that would have on Christian theology. The author Marie I. George summarises his view:

> "On the one hand, the human species would reflect God's goodness in a special way by being unique, while on the other hand, it is befitting to God's goodness that he create more of better creatures. Aquinas leans in the direction of the former view, but realises that the latter could in fact be the case."[13]

So, if we shift our understanding of what it means to be the image of God towards something vocational, this dissolves the potential conflict there with intelligent alien life.

---

[13] George, 2001

Next, we'll explore what implications this alien scenario may have on the doctrine of the incarnation.

Is there an alien Jesus?

"Your own personal Jesus
Someone to hear your prayers
Someone who cares"
- Depeche Mode

Do aliens have their own Jesus, or are they redeemed by ours too? This single question reveals a lot about your understanding of who Jesus is and why he came to Earth.

In C.S. Lewis' book The Voyage of the Dawn Treader, the kingly lion Aslan tells the girl Lucy, "In your world, I have another name. You must learn to know me by that name." In the realm of Narnia, Lucy had become friends with Aslan, a Christ-like figure. But he hinted that he also lived in her world too (our Earth) under a different name.

What makes Christianity distinctive is the claim of the incarnation – the claim that God, in the Son, has taken on human flesh. The roots of this truth always lay hidden in the great monotheistic tradition of Judaism.

There is a mysterious figure called the Angel (messenger) of YHWH, who is referred to 65 times in the Bible. He speaks for YHWH, yet also speaks directly as YHWH, and he carries the name and authority of God Himself. The acts of God are attributed to him, yet he is distinct from God. While Judaism worships only one almighty God, it describes this angel who is YHWH yet is also with YHWH, just as John wrote "the Word was with God, and the Word was God." Sometimes this angel appears in human form, foreshadowing his incarnation as the human that people then called Jesus. Later, New Testament writers and various early church fathers associated YHWH's messenger with Jesus (e.g., 1 Corinthians 10:9).

The prophet Daniel also saw a vision of a human figure ("the son of man") who appears before the almighty God in the same way YHWH is described as appearing – "with the clouds of heaven." This human *was given authority, glory and sovereign power; all nations and peoples of every language worshipped him. His dominion is an everlasting dominion that will not pass away, and his kingdom is one that will never be destroyed"* (Daniel 7:14). Jesus adopted the title "the son of man" for himself, claiming to be this YHWH figure who would receive a kingdom from YHWH.

But it's only in Christianity that the incarnation takes on full resolution. This is a supremely unusual claim. The creator God becomes a creature, yet without ceasing to be God and without overwhelming the integrity of the creature He becomes.

And he became a human.

It *could* be claimed that God gave humanity dominion only over the Earth (though I push back at this claim later in this book), leaving room for alien species elsewhere. But it *couldn't* be claimed that Christianity leaves room for any rival to Jesus' absolute claim of authority over the entire universe.

Colossians 1:15-20 describes:

> *"The Son is the image of the invisible God, the firstborn over all creation. For* **in him all things were created**: *things in heaven and on earth, visible and invisible, whether thrones or powers or rulers or authorities;* **all things have**

> **been created through him and for him**. *He is before all things, and in him all things hold together. And he is the head of the body, the church; he is the beginning and the firstborn from among the dead, so that in everything he might have the supremacy. For God was pleased to have all his fullness dwell in him, and* **through him to reconcile to himself all things**, *whether things on earth or things in heaven, by making peace through his blood, shed on the cross."*

This scripture isn't just referring to Jesus' divinity. As Jesus is "the head of the body, the church" and "the beginning and firstborn from among the dead," by his resurrection, Jesus is the first to fully embody the image-bearing role God conferred on all humanity in Eden.

Jesus is pierced by Jerusalemite nails and impaled on a Roman spear. When he rises, he keeps these glorified wounds and ascends to the Father's right hand, thereby filling the universe (Ephesians 4:10) and reconciling heaven and earth by his human blood (Colossians 1:20).

Then, at the end of the book, the first verse of the Bible is consummated: heaven and earth marry (Revelation 21:2). The metaphor is that Christ marries just one bride made up of all his redeemed and perfected people. The dwelling of God is with humanity on a resurrected earth, and they all live happily ever after.

That's the story. You can dismiss it as impossibly anthropocentric or earth-loving if you like, but to lose these elements is to lose the heart of it.

And crucially for our discussion, Jesus' incarnation as a human has now been made permanent. While he was born with a mortal body, his resurrection body is immortal. *"For* we know that since Christ was raised from the dead, he cannot die again; death no longer has mastery over him. The death he died, he died to sin once for all; but the life he lives, he lives to God." (Romans 6:9-10). Thus, Jesus is permanently human (while also being permanently God) and because he won't die again, he can't die for aliens in another form.

In the orthodox view, Jesus embodies two natures – the human and the divine – as a single person. This belief precludes him from existing in multiple incarnations at once, as that would imply multiple separate identities, each with their unique combination of natures. Consequently, an 'alien Jesus' would be an entirely different entity from the 'human Jesus'. Following his resurrection, the second person of the Trinity has forever adopted a human nature, making it impossible for any transition from one incarnation (divine + human) to another (divine + alien) to occur.

Conversely, in his *Age of Reason,* the American revolutionary Thomas Paine used the supposedly obvious profusion of alien worlds as an argument against the incarnation, and therefore against Christianity:

> *"From whence, then, could arise the solitary and strange conceit, that the Almighty, who had millions of worlds equally dependent on His protection, should quit the care of all the rest, and come to die in our world because they say one man and one woman had eaten an apple! And, on the other hand, are we to suppose that every world in the boundless creation had an Eve, an apple, a serpent and redeemer? In this case, the person who is irreverently called the Son of God, and sometimes God himself, would have nothing else to do than to travel from world to world, in an endless succession of death, with scarcely a momentary interval of life."[14]*

Personally, I believe that this is one line that Christians can't cross without breaking one of the most fundamental cornerstones of their faith: in Christ, God became forever human with a permanent and exclusive union of His divine and human natures. Sorry aliens, no alien Jesus for you.

There's one final sliver of a get-out clause that someone could claim leaves room within Christian orthodoxy for an incarnation of God as an alien for aliens: the idea that the Holy Spirit could be incarnated as an alien species for their redemption. This probably isn't even an option you've considered before, but it's worth being thorough, though I won't spend long on it.

The problem with this concept is that the Holy Spirit indwells believers; He is the one who empowers and communicates the presence of God to us here in this age. Jesus' incarnation seemed to localise him – as a human, Jesus no longer exploits his divine prerogative of omnipresence (Philippians 2:6-8). Surely this same principle would apply to an incarnation of the Spirit – it would similarly localise Him, precluding His indwelling in believers.

Ephesians 1:13-14 explains that the Holy Spirit is given to every believer as a guarantee of their future glorification. This starts as soon as we believe and lasts right until we receive our resurrection inheritance:

> *"**When you believed**, you were marked in [Christ] with a seal, the promised Holy Spirit, who is a deposit guaranteeing our inheritance **until the redemption** of those who are God's possession—to the praise of his glory."*

---

[14] Paine, 1998

So the Holy Spirit can't be incarnated for the redemption of aliens while believers in Jesus live on earth. This would constitute another red line for Christian orthodoxy.

Could God the Father be incarnated? He's no more nor less God than the Son and the Spirit, but I'd say the Father fulfils a different role as the perpetual source of the Son and Spirit, so acts as the one who sends, not the one who is sent.

In any case, it probably wouldn't be necessary for God to have multiple incarnations, as the redemption that Jesus the God-man has achieved as a human being has implications for the whole universe. So next, we'll delve into the topic of redemption.

Redemption for aliens

The question of whether God could have other incarnations on other planets didn't feature much in theological discussions until the 20th century. That's because it was usually assumed that Jesus' act of redemption as a human was sufficient for all creatures everywhere.

Jesuit George Coyne SJ, director of the Vatican Observatory from 1978 to 2006, laid out the question of redemption for our alien peers thus:

"How could he be God and leave extraterrestrials in their sin? After all, He was good to us. Why should He not be good to them? God chose a very specific way to redeem human beings. He sent his only Son, Jesus, to them and Jesus gave up his life so that human beings would be saved from their sin. Did God do this for extraterrestrials?"[5]

While Jesus was crucified as a human specifically so he could atone for the sins of humans, Christianity believes that this great act has cosmic implications. So taking the question seriously, we'll explore the possibilities. Is there hope for our alien peers?

What are our options?

To determine what options would and wouldn't fit within orthodox Christianity, first we have three questions to address:

1. Would our alien peers actually sin?
2. If so, would they be held accountable for that sin?
3. If so, would they be offered redemption?

This creates four options:

	Not offered redemption	Offered redemption
Not sinning	A) Like unfallen angels	n/a
Sinning but not held accountable	B) Like animals	n/a
Sinning and held accountable	C) Like fallen angels	D) Ostensibly incompatible with Christianity

A. They never sin, like holy angels
B. They aren't held accountable for sin, just like alien pets and all non-human life on earth
C. They are held accountable for sin yet they aren't offered redemption, like fallen angels
D. They are held accountable for sin and offered redemption, but we don't know how

---

[15] Dick, 2014, 187

A) Sinless, like holy angels

The whole question of redemption carries an assumption that aliens would need it. One possibility is that they could be technically morally culpable for sin while managing to remain sinless. Perhaps they had their own Garden of Eden moment, but they refused the temptation to rebelliously reach for their own power and wisdom apart from God.

A later director of the Vatican Observatory, José Gabriel Funes, speculated optimistically that:

> *"We human beings might be the lost sheep, the sinners in need of a shepherd. God became man in Jesus to save us. In that case, even if there were other sentient life forms, they might not be in need of redemption. They could have stayed in full harmony with their Creator."*[16]

C.S. Lewis, the author of the Chronicles of Narnia, wrote a less well-known sci-fi trilogy for adults, and I love the richness and originality of those stories.

In the second book, the human character Ransom is brought to the Edenic planet Perelandra (known to us as Venus) to help Tinidril, their alien Eve, resist her own version of temptation. Spoiler alert: Ransom succeeds, she chooses to continue with trusting, humble innocence, and their planet avoids a million years of holocaust and

Perelandra,
C.S. Lewis

malevolent chaos that would have been far worse than any our earth will ever know.

Thomas Aquinas wrote: "the one who is not harmed by

---

[16] Giangravè, 2017

sin, is not in need of redemption. If therefore there would be someone who was not born in original sin, aside from Christ, there would be someone who was not in need of the redemption accomplished by Christ."[17]

So that's the first option: our alien peers never sin, so their redemption isn't even necessary.

But now let's assume that they aren't perfect in everything they do.

B) Sinning but not held accountable

This category is a bit of a misnomer because, technically, animals will be held accountable for killing humans, as Genesis 9:5-6 describes. Yet in that scripture, the consequence of shedding the blood of God's imagers is immediate, and it is to be carried out in this life. This isn't dealt with by Jesus' atonement, and animals probably aren't judged along with humanity, so it isn't pertinent to this point. While animals can do wrong things (e.g. kill a human image of God), they won't be eternally judged for that sin. Animals likely don't have much of an afterlife, though I haven't been there and no one's sent me a postcard from the other side yet.

Hebrews 2 (covered in the next point) describes how Jesus' death as a human achieved redemption for humans alone. Yet because God delegated to humanity (as His imagers) the authority to rule and care for the earth, our sin causes corruption throughout the whole earth. In Romans 8, Paul explains:

> *"For the creation waits in eager expectation for the children of God to be revealed. For the creation was subjected to*

---

[17] George, 2001

frustration, not by its own choice, but by the will of the one
who subjected it, in hope that the creation itself will be
liberated from its bondage to decay and brought into the
freedom and glory of the children of God."
- *Romans 8:19-21*

The passage continues to elaborate that this grand transformation will transpire when God's redeemed humans are unveiled in their gloriously resurrected forms. This event marks the moment when redeemed humanity receives its full inheritance as sons and daughters. The rest of creation will then be swept up with the sons of God into resurrection, setting in motion the emergence of a new heaven and a new earth.

This sequence of resurrection begins with Jesus, the firstborn son, who was the first to be raised. Following this, every individual who joins him through faith will experience their resurrection. This resurrection of redeemed humanity will trigger the renewal of the rest of creation.

This wave of renewal will ripple throughout the cosmos, touching every corner of creation. Every tardigrade, shrew, and llama on Earth, along with hypothetical extraterrestrial life forms like alien algae, will be liberated from the chains of corruption and decay that are synonymous with death. They, too, will partake in this profound resurrection, embracing an existence where death is only a fading shadow. The narrative paints a vivid picture of a universe reborn, pulsating with new life and unfathomable possibilities.

It's worth noting that Paul claims that the fall of humanity affects the whole of creation, not just life on earth. This is the same author who wrote that Jesus is "the firstborn over all creation. For in him all things were created: things in heaven and on earth, visible and invisible, whether thrones or powers or rulers or authorities; all things have been created through him and for him" (Colossians 1:15-16). So when Paul writes "creation," he has everything apart from God in view. If all creation is waiting to be brought into the freedom and glory of redeemed humanity, that suggests that all creation is under humanity in some way. Therefore, our vocation as God's image extends to the whole creation, the whole universe, not just to life on earth.

One time, the famous Catholic writer, theologian, philosopher, and preacher G.K. Chesterton contemplated Christ's death on the cross. It became, in his mind, the most significant act ever carried out in the universe, representing the centre of all space and time. Speaking to a large audience, he mused about the cosmic implications:

"If the inhabitants in all the stars did not see Christ die, if from all worlds they could not behold the dreadful sight, yet they must have heard of it in many a star by this time. Swift spirits have told, in those bright orbs where myriads of unfallen creatures dwell, the story that, on this little dusky planet, sin struggled against incarnate love, and love, to conquer it, did die, and in the dying won the victory. I cannot tell you how many races of intelligent beings there are beside the hierarchy of angels, but it is not at all improbable that there are as many worlds as there are grains of sand upon the seashore, and perhaps every one of these teems with inhabitants more than our earth does; and they have heard, and they keep on hearing, and the news keeps spreading everywhere, that the God, who made them all, took human form, and died to put away human sin."

"And, supposing this is the case, what do you think all these intelligent beings say? It must be that the impression made upon them is that sin is a horrible thing, since it stabs at God himself. All intelligences must also feel that God is just, since he will sooner himself die than let sin go unpunished. It further rings throughout the spheres that God is love, – that he will sooner bleed to death than let his creatures perish; and that here he once proved, in his death, that he was infinite both in his vengeance and his mercy."[18]

There's not a lot of consensus within Christianity as to whether animals will be resurrected when Jesus returns. The pastor John Piper wrote:

"And as I knelt beside the brook
To drink eternal life, I took
A glance across the golden grass,
And saw my dog, old Blackie, fast
As she could come. She leaped the stream—
Almost—and what a happy gleam
Was in her eye. I knelt to drink,
And knew that I was on the brink
Of endless joy."[19]

However, if every animal that ever died were indeed resurrected, we'd need many, many earths to fit them all in. One thing is certain: even if individual creatures aren't resurrected, creation as a whole will be renewed and freed from its "bondage to decay" when humanity, in its redeemed state, resumes its sacred role as the steward of creation again.

---

[18] Spurgeon, 1881
[19] Piper, 1985

In the same way, if any intelligent aliens exist across the vast expanse of our universe, Jesus' death as a human could affect them too. Their species could be renewed and freed from the death and decay brought through the fall of humanity, without individual aliens being judged for their sins.

C) Damned like fallen angels

Angels are in a unique category. Fallen angels were never weakened by doubt nor led astray by anyone else like we are. They had perfect knowledge of God, seeing Him face to face, yet they still chose to hate His transcendence, coveting His throne. Aquinas believed that angels receive their understanding directly from God, and in contemplating the divine essence, they come to know all things. The severity of God's judgement varies according to how much knowledge a person possesses (Luke 12:48), and because angels know so much, their rebellion is final. It constitutes a self-hardening in which angels lock themselves into their cold, dead hatred. Scripture paints a picture of fallen angels as so antithetical to everything good and free that they act perpetually unrepentant. They never show a shred of remorse, only doubling down in their self-deceiving pride whenever the futility of their sin is revealed. Thus, they're not offered redemption because they wouldn't ever accept it.

In the Bible, the writer of the letter to the Hebrews is very clear:

"Since the children have flesh and blood, [Jesus] too shared in their humanity so that by his death he might break the power of him who holds the power of death—that is, the devil— and free those who all their lives were held in slavery by their

*fear of death. For surely **it is not angels he helps**, but Abraham's descendants. For this reason he had to be made like them, **fully human in every way**, in order that he might become a merciful and faithful high priest in service to God, and that he might make atonement for the sins of the people."*
- Hebrews 2:14-17

Note: as Paul describes in Galatians 3:27, in this context Abraham's descendants are everyone who believes in Jesus, children of faith.

So, Jesus doesn't help rescue any angels that sin but only humans, and that's why he became a human. As the ultimate priest for humanity, he represents humanity before God as a flesh-and-blood human, no longer as a disembodied spirit.

It's unlikely that biological intelligent alien peers would display the same self-damning, stubborn pride of demons. It really depends on how much they know of God, but considering this kind of closeness to the divine to be possible starts to shift them from the 'peers' hypothesis into the 'phantoms' hypothesis, which I'll address in part two.

D) Sinning and somehow offered redemption?

At the end of C.S. Lewis' book Perelandra, Ransom has an enrapturing encounter with some planetary spirits in which he finds out that if Tinidril had chosen the way of pride and selfishness, the supreme God would have forged a unique redemption for them. This wouldn't have been achieved through the death of God incarnate but through something unspecified, even more terrible and wonderful

35

than Earth's own, to match the greater evil of fallen Perelandra. This is a tantalising mystery but essentially a "non-answer."

The possibility of extraterrestrial life having its own distinct path to redemption doesn't align comfortably with traditional Christian orthodoxy. A key passage in Hebrews 2 demarcates the boundaries of redemption, suggesting that non-human entities are exempt from direct salvation for accountable sins via Jesus's atoning sacrifice.

In this theological view, redemption through Jesus is an exclusive privilege bestowed upon humanity. As our brother, Jesus serves as our "kinsman redeemer," a term rooted in ancient familial traditions. The kinsman redeemer is one who shoulders the honour and duty of rescuing a kin in need, metaphorically extending a life-saving hand to a relative who is struggling in the stormy sea of life.

Imagine this: Jesus, as our spiritual kinsman, stretches out this hand of redemption, yet it is a hand that reaches specifically for humanity. His redemption is an intimate familial rescue, a unique bond that resonates deeply within the human condition. As it stands, traditional Christian orthodoxy doesn't see Jesus extending this familial redemption to hypothetical alien lifeforms.

Hebrews 2:11 states that "he who sanctifies and those who are sanctified all have one source. That is why he is not ashamed to call them brothers," so everyone Jesus redeems "has the same source" and is "a brother" of Jesus.

One could argue that if God created everything, all aliens have the same source as us, but when this scripture states we have the same source, it describes us as intimate members of the same family. Verse 14 then decisively states "Since the children have flesh and blood, he too shared in their humanity so that by his death he might break the power of him who holds the power of death— that is, the devil." So Jesus redeems only those who share his human flesh and blood.

The enduring mystery

Although the theological roots of redemption through the Messiah are deeply woven into the fabric of even the most ancient scripture, how it was all going to pan out was always a great mystery.

> *"Concerning this salvation, the prophets, who spoke of the grace that was to come to you, searched intently and with the greatest care… Even angels long to look into these things."*
> *- 1 Peter 1:10, 12*

Old Testament scriptures were always clear that the Messiah had to suffer (Luke 24:25-27), yet no one knew how this was going to undo the work of the evil one, kill death and open the way for people from every nation to be reconciled with God.

> *"We declare God's wisdom, a mystery that has been hidden and that God destined for our glory before time began. None of the rulers of this age understood it, for if they had, they would not have crucified the Lord of glory."*
> *- 1 Corinthians 2:7-8*

The mechanics of our own redemption were always a complete mystery right until the powers of darkness found themselves confounded and their claim over humanity broken. So, I'm reluctant to dictate what God can and can't do.

I'll admit that if our alien peers do indeed exist, and if they fear death, if they feel the stab of emotional and intellectual pain, if they wonder at the purpose of life and struggle with sin and suffering, it would be right, and even expected, for the God who has come close to us in Christ to also draw near to them. It would be just the kind of thing He does.

God is love, so He is working to reconcile all things to Himself (Colossians 1:20), as much as possible. By His example, God has revealed that love means willing the good of another for their own sake. The lover longs to take upon themselves the situation of the beloved, to be as intimately united to them in it as possible.

Speaking in 2014 on the concept of inclusion, Pope Francis recounted how Peter was criticised by Jewish believers in Jerusalem when he accepted gentiles. Francis said he would baptise anyone who asked, then took his call for acceptance to its logical extreme, saying he'd even baptise aliens. *"If, for example, tomorrow an expedition of Martians came to us here and one said 'I want to be baptised!', what would happen?... Martians, right? Green, with long noses and big ears, like in children's drawings... When the Lord shows us the way, who are we to say, 'No, Lord, it is not prudent! No, let's do it this way'. Who are we to close doors?"*[20]

Even if extraterrestrials exist, there's nothing that contradicts our history with the human Adam, God putting on human flesh and rescuing us, as one of us.

---

[20] Withnall, 2014

4. PETS AND PEERS: CONCLUDING THOUGHTS

So, do aliens exist? Well, there is no compelling reason to believe they do, and in fact, logic might suggest otherwise. However, for the sake of argument, if biological aliens were discovered, it still shouldn't undermine the Christian faith.

Under a functional interpretation of the image of God, the existence of extraterrestrial beings wouldn't challenge our status as bearers of God's image. Furthermore, they couldn't possess their own incarnation of God; thus, they wouldn't have their own distinct redemption but could be included in the renewal of all things stemming from our redemption.

Regardless of the outcome, "truth cannot contradict truth," so we have nothing to fear. Whatever the relationship between aliens and God may be, it doesn't need to impact our narrative involving Adam and Jesus. Vatican astronomer and theologian Giuseppe Tanzella-Nitti expressed it this way:

> *"Christians do not have to renounce their faith in God just because of new unexpected information of a religious nature regarding extraterrestrial civilizations."*[21]

However, there is still more to consider. What about

---

[21] Giangravè, 2017

39

the presence of phantoms or aliens as entities much closer to what we might perceive as cosmic spirits?

PART 2:

CHRISTIANITY HAS KNOWN ABOUT ALIENS FOR A LONG TIME

1. WHY EVEN?

A significant portion of my writing focuses on Christian Apologetics, which aims to defend the rationality of the Christian faith. But doesn't discussing aliens and UFOs seriously make us seem ridiculous or even irrational? Are we genuinely considering the existence of little green men from Mars? Why write about aliens?

> *"The moment you mention UFO, immediately what comes to mind is little green men, tinfoil hats. That's not at all what we're dealing with."*
> *- Lou Elizondo, former US Pentagon program director*

Modern Christian Apologetics often challenges the assertions of New Atheism, but recent research indicates that there might be a larger and more intriguing subject to engage with. The Pew Research Center recently reported that 29% of US adults identify as atheist, agnostic, or "nothing in particular."[22] However, in a study on alien beliefs conducted last year, they found that 65% of US adults believe intelligent life exists beyond Earth, and 51% of those think UFOs reported by military personnel are evidence of the same.[23] A 2006 research paper revealed that roughly 25% of people claimed to have seen a UFO.[24]

Interestingly, the number of people who believe in aliens aligns closely with belief in God, and this correlation

---

[22] Pew Research Center, 2022
[23] Pew Research Center, 2021
[24] Dewan, 2006

may not be coincidental. Interest in UFOs could represent a form of religious faith, and the appearance of UFOs in our skies might signal the emergence of a new religion.

Therefore, this topic is worth exploring. Contrary to popular assumption, the discovery of alien life would not necessarily destroy Christianity. In part one, I began examining this question by considering two scenarios:

1. Aliens equivalent to our *pets* (inferior extraterrestrial biological organisms)
2. Aliens more like our *peers* (equal or superior extraterrestrial biological organisms)

Now in part two, I will delve into a third premise: aliens as phantoms – entities that are entirely different from us.

These hypothetical phantoms represent interdimensional beings: aliens as visitors from another plane of existence existing alongside ours, rather than traditionally understood biological life from outer space. This third scenario aligns more closely with modern UFOlogy's direction and, as we will discover, resonates more with Christianity's supernatural worldview. Although the alien legend appears to represent a very modern religion, it closely resembles something that has accompanied us for a long time.

However, a word of caution is necessary. You might expect this book to jump to the conclusion that "aliens are demons." As we will see, it is not that simple. Equating UFOs with demons would be overly simplistic without first examining the data and defining our terms. I do not believe that encountering an alien equates to meeting a mischievous red devil in disguise, out on a day trip from tormenting people in hell.

Our modern minds have inherited many confused and one-dimensional ideas, but I contend that the Christian supernatural worldview has much to offer in terms of depth and insight for this third hypothetical scenario – aliens as phantoms.

First, let us lay some groundwork by examining some aspects of UFOlogy's modern history.

Keywords:

- Extraterrestrial: a biological being originating from somewhere in our universe other than earth
- Interdimensional: a being originating from another realm of space or time
- Ultraterrestrial: a superior nonhuman supernatural being indigenous to earth
- UAP: Unidentified Anomalous Phenomena, a new and broader term replacing UFO
- AATIP: Advanced Aerospace Threat Identification Program

2. INTERESTING MURMURINGS FROM US GOVERNMENT

In December 2017, The New York Times published a groundbreaking report[25] on a secret $22 million project run by the US Pentagon called the Advanced Aerospace Threat Identification Program. The report included two videos named "FLIR" and "GIMBAL," after the equipment used to record them. These videos purportedly showed encounters that Navy jets from the Nimitz and Theodore Roosevelt aircraft carriers had in 2004 with unusually shaped objects flying at incredible speeds (later referred to as UAP). In March the following year, The Washington Post published another video,[26] titled "GOFAST," which depicted a high-speed object tracked by an F/A-18 Super Hornet military jet.

The military and intelligence community were astonished by these objects' apparent capabilities. As The Washington Post described:

> *"According to incident reports and interviews with military personnel, these vehicles descended from altitudes higher than 60,000 feet at supersonic speeds, only to suddenly stop and hover as low as 50 feet above the ocean. The United States possesses nothing capable of such feats."[27]*

---

[25] Kean, 2017
[26] Mellon, 2018
[27] Mellon, 2018

Cmdr David
Fravor

Multiple state-of-the-art radar systems aboard ships and aircraft simultaneously monitored these objects. Navy pilot and Black Aces squadron commander David Fravor[28] intercepted the UAP recorded in the Nimitz encounter (seen in the FLIR video) and later described the object as having no discernible control surfaces or means of propulsion. Witnesses reported bizarrely simple shapes, such as tic-tac shapes and even a cube within a semi-transparent bubble. Sensors often recorded these objects' temperatures as resting at the ambient air temperature, with none of the expected heat exhaust coming from a jet.

Pilot Chad Underwood, who filmed the famous "FLIR" video in a second wave of jets behind Fravor, stated:

Pilot Chad Underwood

"It was just behaving in ways that aren't physically normal. That's what caught my eye. Because aircraft, whether they're manned or unmanned, still have to obey the laws of physics. They have to have some source of lift, some source of propulsion. The Tic Tac was not doing that. It was going from like 50,000 feet to, you know, a hundred feet in like seconds, which is not possible."[29]

Radar operators reported tracking one of the UAPs in the Nimitz incident dropping from the sky at over 30 times the speed of sound. Fravor likened their rapid side-to-side movements to a ping-pong ball. Radar operators on

---

[28] Blumenthal, 2017
[29] Phelan, 2019

46

the USS Princeton, part of the Nimitz carrier group, tracked an object accelerating from a standing position to cover 60 miles (96 km) in a minute – an astonishing 3,600 mph (5,800 km/h).

In June 2021, the Office of the Director of National Intelligence published a basic report on UAPs. It stated: "A majority of UAP were registered across multiple sensors, including radar, infrared, electro-optical, weapon seekers, and visual observation."[30]

It is certainly healthy to approach claimed UFO sightings with scepticism, but these accounts are not being spun by amateurs and spread by gossip; they are the testimonies of trained and experienced observers corroborated with multi-sensor data. This lends them a degree of credibility that merits consideration.

The assessment of military top brass

Since the revelatory New York Times article, the former director of the Pentagon's AATIP (Advanced Aerospace Threat Identification Program), Lue Elizondo, resigned from his role in protest over a lack of transparency about "the phenomenon" (as it has come to be known) within the

Luis Elizondo

intelligence community. In interviews, he subsequently detailed these entities' extraordinary apparent abilities:

"Imagine a technology that can do 600-700 G forces, [for reference, a trained human pilot can endure 10 Gs for a few seconds before they begin to pass out] that can fly at

---

[30] Office of the Director of National Intelligence, 2021

13,000mph, that can evade radar and that can fly through air, water and possibly space. And oh, by the way, has no obvious signs of propulsion, no wings, no control surfaces, and yet can still defy the natural effects of earth's gravity. That's precisely what we're seeing… The government has already stated for the record that they're real. I'm not telling you that, the United States government is telling you that."

These few publicised sightings are not isolated; it is just that data is rarely released to the public. NASA Administrator and Senator Bill Nelson stated:

"Now I know what you've seen is what those Navy pilots saw in 2004 and there have been some 300 sightings since then. I've talked to those pilots, and they know they saw something, their radars locked on to it, it was here on the surface then all of a sudden it's there. And they don't know what it is, and we don't know what it is."[31]

Due to the massive stigma surrounding the idea of believing in "little green men from Mars," many pilots who encounter anomalous "bogies" while on active duty simply keep their sightings to themselves for fear of being signed off work as unhinged.[32]

Not just foreign tech

So could this simply represent encounters with incredibly advanced foreign human technology? Authorities in the US intelligence community don't seem to think so. Elizondo explained how the historical nature

---

[31] Nelson, 2021
[32] Rogan, 2022

of the phenomenon invalidates that idea:

"When you go through the historical documentation… we've been seeing this technology for decades. When you compare that to where we were, say, in the late 1940s and 50s, we were just exploring and learning the secrets of the atom, we had just entered the jet age, and we hadn't even been into space. And yet these technologies were outperforming anything and everything that we have. So if this is some form of adversarial [human] technology that's been around for 70 years, this would be considered probably the worst intelligence failure my country has ever experienced, perhaps even eclipsing that of 9/11."[33]

US Senator Mitt Romney concurs:

"Well I don't believe that they're coming from foreign adversaries, if they were, that would suggest that they have a technology which is in a whole different sphere than anything we understand, and frankly China and Russia just aren't there."

Christopher Mellon, former Deputy Assistant Secretary of Defense for Intelligence, elaborated:

"We monitor the Chinese and Russians very closely, very carefully. We spend (I think the unclassified figure is) $70 billion per year on intelligence programs. And it would be very surprising, and stunning, if they had independently developed technology that was that far ahead of everything else and everyone else, somehow secretly. It doesn't seem likely, and we don't think that's the case. More likely something

---

[33] Elizondo, 2021

else."[34]

(Note: For an excellent summary of UAP related testimony from top US Officials, see *The UAP / UFO Video for the Rest of Us: US Officials on the Record*, 2022 on YouTube.)

In the US, former Presidents, former directors of the CIA, former directors of National Intelligence, former and current members of Congress, and the current administrator for NASA have confirmed that the phenomenon is real and not easily explainable.

The five observables, and other studies

The Pentagon's AATIP program identified five consistent characteristics of the phenomenon, as Elizondo describes:

1. **Antigravity lift:**
   No discernible means of propulsion, they appear to rise up without wings or jets
2. **Sudden and instantaneous acceleration:**
   Accelerating and changing direction at speeds that would immediately crush human occupants
3. **Hypersonic velocities without signatures:**
   No sonic booms, none of the common supersonic vapour trails, no splash when entering water, no air cavitation underwater
4. **Low observability, or cloaking:**
   Sometimes they're visible on radar but not to the eye, sometimes they appear surrounded by a

[34] The U.S. Military Is Growing Concerned About UFOs. Should We Worry?, 2022

visible glow or haze, sometimes they appear to
blip out of existence

5. **Trans-medium travel:**
Seamlessly transitioning between space, air and
underwater

In response to the increased attention given to the
phenomenon over the last five years, in May 2022, the US
held its first congressional hearing on UAPs in 50 years.
The Department of Defense also relaunched its official
investigation office,[35] and NASA is joining in with its own
study. None of these efforts would really make sense if the
technology was the result of secret US black projects.

Furthermore, in August of 2022, Ukrainian researchers
conducted an independent study of UAP,[36] managing to
capture video using cameras designed for monitoring
meteors in the daytime sky. They break down their
observations of UAPs into two primary categories, which
they call "Cosmics" and "Phantoms." "We note that
Cosmics are luminous objects, brighter than the
background of the sky." Whereas "Phantoms are dark
objects, with contrast from several to about 50 percent."

"Phantoms are observed in the troposphere at
distances up to 10 – 12 km," the researchers state,
estimating their size to be 3–12 m and capable of speeds of
as much as 9 miles per second (33,000 mph). Their
synchronised camera systems also detected an entity at an
altitude of 727 miles (1,170 km), well beyond the Kármán
line that traditionally delineates the edge of space at 62
miles (100 km) above sea level.

---

[35] Hanks, 2022
[36] Hanks, 2022

The only substantial rebuttal of their findings so far, by the theoretical physicist and astrophysicist Avi Loeb, argued that the distances (and therefore speeds and sizes) must have been overestimated by an order of magnitude. He writes: "their bow shock in the Earth's atmosphere would have generated a bright fireball with an easily detectable optical luminosity." But this objection ignores the common third observation described by AATIP - hypersonic velocities without signatures. What physical object can rip through the air at 33,000 mph (53,100 km/h) without causing a fireball? Supposedly, no physical object can, but apparently that doesn't stop something from doing so.

Given the wealth of corroborative evidence and meticulously documented reports from credible military and intelligence communities, it may be time for us to abandon our scepticism regarding "the phenomenon" simply because it doesn't conform to our preconceived notions of how physical entities ought to behave. Instead of dismissing the enigmatic, we could potentially unlock new realms of understanding by revisiting our perception of its physicality.

Aliens and Christianity: Threat or Vindication?

3. BEYOND PHYSICAL

So-called antigravity lift and incredible speeds are impressive, but to me, the most intriguing of the 'five observables' is the lack of the usual hypersonic signatures associated with physical objects. When an object travels faster than the sound it creates, the pressure waves stack together behind it, creating a sonic boom that can be heard by a stationary observer. Similarly, when objects travel underwater, pockets of water vapour are formed when the water behind an object drops below the liquid's natural vapour pressure – this is called cavitation.

What's truly puzzling, though, is that despite these objects darting through air and water at breathtaking velocities, they can do so without leaving sonic booms and underwater cavitation in their wake. Ordinarily, any object moving through water would leave behind a short-lived trail of cavitation bubbles. Similarly, when conventional objects fly at supersonic speeds, they displace air, and this displacement creates a pressure wave that releases as a sonic boom. Yet, these standard physical markers are missing.

So, according to the most highly attested reports tracked on multiple radar systems with observations corroborated by highly trained and experienced military personnel, what we have is a phenomenon that:

    1.   Is apparently under intelligent control, responding

Aidan Ashby

to the movements of aircraft

2. Can sometimes be seen by the human eye and recorded by radar systems
3. Displays extraordinary behaviour not explainable by any known or reasonable modern human technology
4. Appears to accelerate at speeds that would turn biological beings to mush
5. Can avoid interacting with physical mediums of air and water while travelling through them

There clearly is a physical manifestation associated with the phenomenon in the form of electromagnetic radiation that can be visible to cameras and radar sensors. After the Nimitz encounter, Fravor also recounted seeing the sea foaming like it was boiling while a 40-foot tic tac shaped craft jumped around erratically 50 feet (15 metres) in the air over it.

But this physicality seems to be entirely negotiable to whatever is behind the UAPs. While they can sometimes be seen, their low observability is noticed often enough for it to be labelled a common observable (a confusing twist of irony). Sometimes people will see objects but they won't be picked up by cameras, or sometimes cameras or radar will while they remain invisible to people. Additionally, there are repeated reports of similar anomalous objects splitting, merging and changing shape while in flight.

Not only is this phenomenon far beyond the capabilities of our technology, it is far beyond the normal limitations of our physical world. They disobey the rules of light, appearing when they want. They don't interact with physical mediums such as air and water. Furthermore, they move without discernible propulsion and they act as if gravity doesn't exist. I think we can call UAPs "physically impervious" in that while they can adopt physical manifestation and affect the world around them (whether by making themselves visible, leaving indentations on the ground or causing the sea to boil), they don't behave like classic physical objects. Interacting with physical matter is entirely optional to them.

What's perhaps more eerie than an apparent lack of physicality is that in one encounter, after buzzing two Navy jets, one of these UAPs shot off at immense speed before reappearing, stationary, at a prearranged aerial meeting point known only by the pilots and ground crew (known as a CAP point),[37] like it was waiting for them to arrive.

Award-winning Stanford University immunologist and UAP researcher Garry Nolan articulated this point of view:

"Now I don't know whether it's a technology per se, because I'm leaving open the idea that it's some form of consciousness that is non-material… I know this all sounds absolutely crazy, but if you've seen the things that I've seen, you would only be able to come to a similar conclusion."

---

[37] HISTORY, 2019

4. LET'S NOT LOSE OUR HEADS JUST YET

If you're anything like me, you're probably finding this all a bit strange and hard to follow. Let's take a step back.

Clearly, we shouldn't be too quick to draw conclusions. There is a glut of alien-enthusiast literature that is simply utter nonsense. I don't believe Illuminati reptilians walk among us. I don't believe the Nazis have continued to build cities inside our hollow Earth or on the far side of the moon.

When ordinary citizens report seeing strange things in the sky, they often inadvertently add a layer of interpretation to their descriptions. This rationalisation is part of our continual attempt to understand what we experience. When faced with the unknown, we search for a category to make it feel a little less threatening. But these hastily devised layers of imposed meaning can get in the way of objective thinking and lead down some blind alleys. A public that is bombarded by films and TV shows featuring physical biological aliens visiting us from distant star systems will more readily interpret aerial phenomena through that lens. Cognitive bias then sets in, as people more easily accept interpretations that align with their preconceived ideas and reject those that challenge them. And yes, this bias is definitely present in more religiously minded people too.

So the language we use when describing and discussing alleged experiences is important. In this book, I'll use a few theological words that may provoke certain impressions, but some of our culture's common associations with these words will be problematic. I'll seek to explain as I go to avoid either forcing too shallow a theology onto the phenomenon or dismissing any theological interpretations out of hand.

In modern UFOlogy, there's been a subtle yet noteworthy shift in language too: nowadays people no longer talk about UFOs (Unidentified Flying Objects), now it's UAPs (Unidentified Aerial Phenomena, or the more domain agnostic Unidentified Anomalous Phenomena). This shift of language from Objects to Phenomena reflects the idea that thinking of it as entirely or solely physical in nature doesn't fully accord with what is actually being observed. Or at least calling the phenomenon "objects" may negatively bias people's interpretations of events toward something purely physical, even if not prosaic. Many reports picked up by the military seem to exhibit an uneasy semi-physicality – having measurable physical effects while still contravening common laws of physics.

According to a report produced by the US ODNI (Office of the Director of National Intelligence),[38] out of 144 reports of the phenomenon spotted by military planes from 2004 to 2021, only one could be explained. It's worth noting that this applies only to these military sightings; I suspect the vast majority of sightings by the public are misidentifications or hoaxes. But a minority of unexplained sightings remain, and if even one genuinely displays some characteristics claimed, that changes everything.

---

[38] Kube & Edelman, 2021

5. EMBRACING 'THE WOO'

Whenever someone first starts looking into stories of aliens and UFOs, it isn't long before they encounter what's been called the "woo" aspect. This is the domain of the paranormal, the weird and the crackpot. It can be very off-putting, but as Aristotle wrote, "it is the mark of an educated mind to be able to entertain a thought without accepting it."

Some people persist in UFOlogical research while attempting to completely ignore the preternatural. This "nuts and bolts" approach seeks theories for the conceptual mechanics of supposed extraterrestrial craft. However, in this field, no worthwhile thinking can be done without taking the paranormal into consideration, as it's such a constant feature.

The researcher Josef Allen Hynek called this persistent aspect of the phenomenon "high strangeness." He was an astronomer, professor and chairman of the astronomy department at Northwestern University, and later a ufologist. He served as a scientific advisor to the US Air Force under three UFO-related projects from 1947 to 1969 (Project Sign, Project Grudge, and Project Blue Book). In total, he studied UFOs for 40 years. In his first book, he published the "Close Encounter" scale he had developed to better catalogue UFO reports. He later acted as a consultant for the 1977 UFO film *Close Encounters of the Third Kind*, named after a level of his scale.

Initially a hard sceptic in regard to the phenomenon, he considered the whole alien question to be a fad that would soon pass. The Air Force tasked him with debunking all reports passed to the military and reassuring the public that they all had prosaic natural or man-made explanations. However, he

J. Allen Hynek

became increasingly suspicious of the a priori conclusions and lack of scientific rigour in the Air Force's debunking. This journey from hard sceptic to questioning believer is a journey that other journalists and researchers, such as Ross Coulthart, George Knapp, Eric Weinstein and others, have travelled in more recent times.

Over time, Hynek also became increasingly suspicious of the extraterrestrial hypothesis, the idea that these encounters represent biological beings that have travelled here from vast distances across space. What's interesting to note, however, is that his incredulity didn't primarily stem (as it often does) from the difficulty of interstellar travel but on the reported behaviour of these entities:

> *"A few good sightings a year, over the world, would bolster the extraterrestrial hypothesis—but many thousands every year? From remote regions of space? And to what purpose? To scare us by stopping cars, and disturbing animals, and puzzling us with their seemingly pointless antics?"[39]*

The repeatedly super-physical behaviour of reports also stood out to him:

> *"If you object, I ask you to explain – quantitatively, not qualitatively – the reported phenomena of materialization*

---

[39] Stringfield, 1978, 40-42

*and dematerialization, of shape changes, of the noiseless
hovering in the Earth's gravitational field, accelerations that
– for an appreciable mass – require energy sources far beyond
present capabilities – even theoretical capabilities, the well-
known and often reported E-M (electro-magnetic interference)
effect, the psychic effects on percipients, including purported
telepathic communications."[40]*

Furthermore, Hynek claimed these experiences sometimes had deep spiritual impacts on experiencers:

*"There are people who have had UFO experiences who've
claimed to have developed psychic ability. There have been
reported healings in close encounters and there have been
reported cases of precognition, where people had foreknowledge
or forewarning that they were going to see something. There
has been a change of outlook, a change of philosophy of
persons' lives… I feel that to some extent it may be a
conditioning process."[41]*

Of course, considering the nature of encounters led him to also contemplate the very nature of our reality, as photojournalist Douglas Curran wrote:

*"Hynek submitted that perhaps UFOs were part of a
parallel reality, slipping in and out of sequence with our own.
This was a hypothesis that obviously pained him as an
empirical scientist. Yet after 30 years of interviewing
witnesses and investigating sighting reports, radar contacts,
and physical traces of saucer landings no other hypothesis
seemed to make sense to him."[42]*

---

[40] Stringfield, 1978, 44
[41] Hynek, 1978
[42] Curran, 1985

He later referred to the phenomenon as a kind of spiritual technology. "I hold it entirely possible," he said, "that a technology exists, which encompasses both the physical and the psychic, the material and the mental."[43]

When the world-renowned Swiss psychologist Carl Jung considered the UFO phenomenon, he also pondered its strange association between the physical and the psychological:

> "I have followed up the literature as much as possible and it looks to me as if something were seen and even confirmed by radar, but nobody knows exactly what is seen… there is an overwhelming material pointing to their legendary or mythological aspect. As a matter of fact the psychological aspect is so impressive, that one almost must regret that the UFOs seem to be real after all."[44]

UFO researcher and author John Keel notes in his book Operation Trojan Horse:

> "The UFOs do not seem to exist as tangible, manufactured objects. They do not conform to the natural laws of our environment. They seem to be nothing more than transmogrifications tailoring themselves to our abilities to understand. The thousands of contacts with these entities indicate that they are liars and put-on artists. The UFO manifestations seem to be, by and large, merely minor variations of the age-old demonological phenomenon. Officialdom may feel that if we ignore them long enough, they will go away altogether, taking their place with the vampire myths of the Middle Ages."[45]

---

[43] Fuller, 1980, 164-165
[44] Marshall, 2013

It's interesting to note that by the time Keel wrote this, he wasn't strictly a theist, so his assessment of the phenomenon as "the age-old demonological phenomenon" isn't the result of cognitive bias causing him to seek support for his Christian worldview.

Sometimes different bystanders see different things, and sometimes what they photograph is different from what they see. There doesn't appear to be any rhyme or reason to it. What's consistent isn't the physicality of these things; it's the ideas that they're conveying and the covert, shifty way they glide around the edges of our perception.

It's almost as if they're projecting impressions directly into people's minds, like a virtual reality being directly imposed on people.

Beyond the bizarre optional-physicality that UAPs display, there's another characteristic of the phenomenon that's more extraordinary — its link to consciousness. And for that, we'll start by considering abductions.

Abductions

There are many stories of alien abduction in circulation. These stories are so incredibly outlandish, many of them can sound simply too fantastical to accept. In this section, we'll assess the contents and claims of abduction reports not to argue for their veracity but to see what we can learn about the source of the abduction stories.

John Mack, an atheist, psychiatrist and former professor at Harvard Medical School, studied the stories of people who had claimed to have been abducted. "With abductees," he writes, "the only thing that presents itself in

---

[45] Keel, 2015

this way is real experience. It's not imagination, not lies, people are suffering from PTSD." According to Mack, as these people faced their stories in therapy, they underwent "feelings of terror, rage and grief as intense as any I have encountered as a psychiatrist."[46] But it was even tougher for them to overcome what he calls ontological shock: "the bleak realisation that what they have experienced actually occurred and that reality as they have defined it is forever altered."

I don't doubt that some people go through something that they sincerely interpret as alien visitations, abductions and communication with species from beyond Earth. However, to claim people have genuinely traumatic experiences is one thing, but to trust every interpretation of these experiences is another. Raw experience and interpretation are two different things.

Let's start with one key claim of alien abduction proponents, taking it as true, to see how the logic plays out on its own terms. Many stories involve telepathy, and some claim aliens insert banal false memories to suppress true memories of the events. In this scenario, the true memories of someone's abduction remain hidden in their brain, only retrievable through hypnosis.

Now, if we assume this assessment that an advanced intelligence is able to remotely alter people's minds is correct, we'd then have no reason to believe the entire abduction "memory" wasn't itself a false memory being implanted in someone's mind. This would apply whether they underwent hypnosis or not.

And instead of shedding light on the real events, hypnotherapy further muddies the water. The

[46] Rae, 1994

trustworthiness of memories supposedly retrieved under hypnosis has been widely and repeatedly challenged. Testimony gathered while under hypnosis is considered too unreliable to be accepted as evidence in UK courts. And in fact, if it is true that entities seek to alter people's minds remotely, the time people are most vulnerable to psychological manipulation is while they are undergoing hypnotherapy, so that would be the more reasonable idea.

Of course, abduction stories do come with a sliver of corroborating evidence, most commonly two-fold: missing time and miniature bodily implants. What must be noted is how scant these are for the outside observer – the first could be a continuation of psychological manipulation, and nothing has ever been proven about the source of the second. They offer just enough data to cultivate the already convinced, but not enough to convince the sceptic.

Purported miniature implants found in people's bodies after abduction events have been likened to tags that wildlife biologists attach to animals as part of their scientific studies, as if this is evidence the phenomenon means no harm. But does tagging an albatross or whale make it suffer an existential crisis or develop a new religion? If implants associated with induced abduction memories are genuine, the psychological impact and philosophical messaging frequently associated with abduction reports lead me to believe implants likely serve as a token, or relic, to reinforce belief. They're an influence mechanism, if real.

But I believe we shouldn't simply mark this one as debunked and get an easy night's sleep. Even in my critical assessment, I assumed (for argument's sake) there was substance to one aspect of the reports, so some of it remains unsettled. Whether abduction reports are genuine memories of past events or falsely implanted narratives, what's striking is that conventional hallucinations rarely repeat such specific details between experiencers. What's striking about abduction reports is how detailed, story-like, and uniform across witnesses they are. So, whatever your position on abductions, their cause still appears unconventional, so we should still assess their contents for clues. Researchers such as folklorist Thomas Bullard[47] argue that most abduction accounts commonly feature events (and this is going to sound very far-fetched) that run along the following lines:

1. **Capture**: The abductee is forcibly taken from terrestrial surroundings to an apparent alien spacecraft

2. **Examination**: Invasive medical or scientific procedures are performed on the abductee

3. **Conference**: The abductors speak to the abductee

4. Tour: The abductees are given a tour of their captors' vessel

5. **Loss of Time**: Abductees rapidly forget the majority of their experience

6. **Return**: The abductees are returned to earth, occasionally in a different location from where they were allegedly taken, with new injuries or dishevelled clothing

7. **Theophany**: The abductee has a profound mystical experience, accompanied by a feeling of oneness with God or the universe

8. **Aftermath**: The abductee must cope with the

---

[47] Pritchard, 1994, 72-74

psychological, physical, and social effects of the experience

Additionally, abduction experiences very commonly involve supernatural elements, such as apparent out-of-body experiences, entities appearing through bedroom walls, and experiencers being taken out of their body and floated through a solid wall or window towards a craft.

"Many abductees, for example, will report that space-time as we know it collapses during their experiences. If you ask them, for example, 'Well, where did this happen?' they may reply, 'Well, it's really not in time and space as we know it.' Those of us who are trained in the Western worldview have no way to deal with that, and even most physicists have no place for such ideas. The abductees speak of 'other dimensions' from which they sense that the beings come, or they say they are taken to another dimension."[48]

Abductees are commonly told they are special, chosen for a breeding program or given access to secret knowledge. The combination of a secret encounter with reassurances the person is special is classic grooming behaviour. Even just the word "abduct" shows how problematic this phenomenon is, to put it mildly. When a person abducts a child, we call that kidnapping and lock them away in prison.

While abduction reports are certainly very difficult to corroborate, their frequently traumatic elements are the most compelling data in support of the idea that the phenomenon represents something "demonic."

---

[48] Mack et al., 1993

The occult

For many years, there has been a close relationship between UFOlogy and the occult. The term "occult" etymologically signifies "hidden from view," and UFOs are hidden from view if they are anything: remember that fourth observable – low observability, or cloaking?

As we consider UFOlogy and the occult, there are two people I want to bring to your attention – Jack Parsons and Aleister Crowley.

Born in 1914, Jack Parsons grew up fascinated with science fiction and the idea that humanity could one day explore the stars. He constantly experimented with small rockets at home with a friend, blasting craters in his backyard. As a schoolboy, these attempts became such an

Jack Parsons

obsession his mother had to move him around schools, his grades suffering until he was finally expelled for blowing up a toilet. Managing to get a job at a chemical production factory which specialised in gunpowder, he poured his newfound money and energy into his dream.

Parsons formed a group with friends from a public college, and they called themselves GALCIT Rocket Research Project, seeking to perfect the chemical compositions needed to fuel a rocket that could escape Earth's gravity. Despite their name, they soon earned the nickname The Suicide Squad for their near-death experiences with explosives, as they moved their expanding projects into the LA desert in an area called the Devil's Gate Dam.

They successfully created a JATO (jet-assisted take-off) system which helped overloaded aircraft into the air. This got the attention of the US Air Force, earning them a grant. Soon, the government hired Parsons and friends to form the Jet Propulsion Laboratory. This facility would eventually constitute the foundation of NASA.

By day, Parsons seemed to be a man of science and logic. Little did his friends and family know, by night he was engaging in magic rituals in hopes that spiritual entities would help him successfully develop rocket technology. Parsons met the magician Aleister Crowley and became deeply involved in the occult. They believed in an esoteric system called Thelema. Their mantra was "do what thou wilt," expressing their motivation to manifest their desires into reality through magic.

Aleister Crowley

Crowley had been brought up in a deeply religious Quaker Christian home. While studying at Cambridge University, he wholly rejected his Christian upbringing, revolting against it so thoroughly he deliberately threw himself into what he considered to be the most directly anti-God, namely the "demonic." Crowley fully embraced this identity, calling himself "the beast" and attempting to summon powerful demons to come to his aid.

In 1917, Crowley believed he had contacted an extraterrestrial intelligence he called "Lam" through a ritual called "Amalantrah Working," which supposedly allowed people to contact beings from outer space and across dimensions. Crowley's concept of Lam is difficult to pin down – on

Illustration:
Lam

one hand, the preternatural creature supposedly lived on the dark side of Mars, but others claim it also represented a manifestation of some future exalted state of Crowley's human mind. After this encounter, he drew the creature, and this visage has since been linked strongly to later encounters with "greys."

Other occultists have described encounters with this same type of creature:

> *"The classic grey alien contact or experience is extreme terror… It's a very cold, mechanical kind of computer-like intelligence. It's what we perceive as artificial because it's not incarnated and it never was. So it doesn't have empathy or doesn't relate to that at all."*[49]

While their occultic system, Thelema, has plenty of spooky and paranormal elements, it's not too far from many new age beliefs and modern-day publications like The Secret, which calls the concept "the law of attraction."

The kind of magic practitioners of Thelema engaged in went well beyond card tricks and escape artistry: they did

---

[49] Armstrong, 2012

sex magic. Parsons soon became the leader of his own group, and they would hold ritual orgies at his mansion. When his wife left him, he started an open relationship with his sister-in-law Sara Hollister, who was also deeply engrossed in Thelema.

Eventually, Parsons' sex addiction no longer satisfied him, so he experimented with drugs to heighten the experience and to strengthen the power of his rituals, in the end becoming addicted to heroin. At one of his meetings, he and Hollister met the science fiction writer L. Ron Hubbard. Parsons was thrilled to meet someone who wrote in such detail about space travel, so he invited Hubbard to join them regularly. Hubbard would eventually go on to marry Hollister, developing the pseudoscientific Dianetics with her as he created the cult of Scientology.

Inspired by Crowley, Parsons believed he could summon a goddess called Babalon, the embodiment of the feminine archetype, a symbol of sexually free women and the mother of the earth. In 1946, he asked his followers to participate in a ritual called "Babalon Working," which sought to call forth this scarlet woman (as described in Revelation 17:3-6) in bodily form, to give birth to the moonchild by immaculate conception. This child could be raised to aspire to reach the stars instead of holding on to the comforts of earth.

Hubbard claimed to channel the voice of Babalon, and soon after the initial rituals, Parsons met a new girlfriend and considered her to be the manifestation of Babalon. However, no moonchild was born. Perhaps, in a way, they did metaphorically call Babalon and the moonchild forth for future generations of humanity as the following decades did, in fact, play out according to their two symbols of sexual anarchism (Babalon) and stellar ambition (the moonchild). The year after Babalon Working saw rumours of an alien spacecraft crash at Roswell, New Mexico, then in 1955, the US entered the space race. Then in the 1960s, hippies spread the 'free love' movement that Parsons had hoped for, and at the end of the decade, the entire world turned on their TVs to watch the first man step on the moon.

Parsons, in his lifetime, attributed his advancements in rocket science not just to his rigorous academic pursuits, but also to his occult practices. He believed that his engagement with the esoteric had a profound impact on his scientific achievements. Following his death, in a gesture acknowledging his contribution to the field of rocket propulsion, NASA named a lunar crater after him. Fittingly or ironically, depending on one's perspective, this crater is located on the far side of the moon, traditionally referred to as the "dark side" - a poetic nod, perhaps, to Parsons' complex and controversial legacy.

6. ASSESSING COMMON HYPOTHESES

So, to summarise our assessment of alien studies (for want of a better term), three aspects support the conclusion that the alien phenomenon (whatever it is) is essentially supernatural:

1. **Technology**: measured observations of entities under intelligent control that aren't subject to the constraints imposed by the laws of physics on physical matter
2. **Encounters**: common paranormal thread in encounters and an otherwise inexplicable link to consciousness, e.g. remote mental manipulation
3. Ties between explicitly **occultic practices** and alien/UFO experiences

Furthermore, we must consider what motivation the phenomenon could have to act the way it does. This aspect is the least considered but possibly the most important.

While not all experiences with the phenomenon leave people traumatised (and some people report positive encounters), harmful encounters reveal the nature of at least some of what lies behind the phenomenon. The abusive nature of abduction experiences and shifty, covert character of appearances show at least some of it is malevolent and deliberately deceptive.

There are many interesting hypotheses proposed to explain the phenomenon:

- All a hoax or misidentification of prosaic objects
- Purely psychological, either individual hallucination or the manifestation of a collective unconscious
- Advanced human technology: secret weapons programs or a hidden advanced breakaway human society
- Biological extraterrestrial visitors from outer space
- Time-travelling humans from the future, perhaps conducting research, perhaps tourism
- Interdimensional: beings originating from another realm of space or time
- Ultraterrestrial: superior nonhuman supernatural beings indigenous to earth

Indeed, one might wonder why we label it as a single phenomenon, rather than breaking it down into separate phenomena, each with their own unique explanation. There's no denying that there have been ample hoaxes, numerous videos of bugs mistaken for distant, large objects, and far too much credulity. It's also true that people can experience hallucinations or delusions, and many reported UFOs likely have mundane explanations, like Mylar balloons or other airborne debris.

However, if even a single credible account exists that amalgamates the three aforementioned features, we are faced with a significant puzzle to decipher. In reality, there isn't just one such account, there are many. These reports aren't just random anecdotes; they come from trained, reliable observers, often corroborated by technological data. Their collective existence suggests a tangible phenomenon that warrants serious and thorough investigation. This is more than mere conjecture or fanciful tales – it's a mystery that continues to defy conventional understanding, calling for focused research.

The most popular conclusion of modern UFOlogy

The space race of 1955–1975 between the USSR and the USA captivated the world with regard to space travel. The possibility of encountering alien races from distant worlds seemed within humanity's grasp. Movies, books, and television shows have reinforced the idea that if we are to encounter non-human intelligences, they will be biological entities from distant worlds. It's no wonder, then, that most of us have naturally come to expect that any non-terrestrial intelligences in the universe would be biological extraterrestrials.

However, over the last few decades, there has been a significant shift in the UFO community. It began with prominent researchers like J. Allen Hynek, Jacques Vallée and others becoming increasingly sceptical of the extraterrestrial hypothesis, eventually publicly preferring the interdimensional hypothesis. This theory suggests that these phenomena may originate from other dimensions or realms of existence, rather than distant planets. Over time, this view has gained considerable traction, leading to a general shift away from the extraterrestrial hypothesis towards the interdimensional or ultraterrestrial hypotheses.

The ultraterrestrial hypothesis is close enough to the interdimensional for both to be considered as one, as it is identical in every way except that it posits the other realm(s) exist spatially connected to us on Earth. This is somewhat reminiscent of the film 'Midnight Special' starring Michael Shannon.

At the start of part two, I set out to explore a third alien scenario – aliens as phantoms rather than pets or peers. The reason I've taken the time to describe modern developments in UFOlogy is because the stories being told and conclusions of major researchers in the field fit quite well with this scenario, as many enthusiasts now acknowledge.

> "It's not about $22 million and the Pentagon has a UFO program, it's about there's an entity out there. There's some kind of non-human intelligence that's living with us on this f*ing planet!"[50]

Spirits, angels and demons?

At the start of part one, I warned that it would be premature to jump to the conclusion that "aliens are demons" without first defining what we mean by both those terms. Our understanding of the supernatural has been filtered through so much clutter that we need to go back to square one to really think things through clearly.

The approach of placing categories against each other in unfamiliar ways can be helpful. For example, considering the proposition "architecture is mathematics" helps us consider architecture in a new way. Similarly, it's helpful for secular thinkers to consider the proposition "aliens are demons", but equally helpful for Christians to consider the proposition "demons are aliens". As a Christian, I'm well aware that when we talk about angels and demons, we really don't know much of what we're

---

[50] Jim Semivan, 2022, from 41:10

talking about.

People who are interested in aliens generally claim to be open-minded to all interpretations of the phenomenon. They like to think they're tolerant of fringe ideas that most people on the street would scoff at. But I've found it surprising how closed-minded these same people can be when someone proposes the idea that aliens are demons. "Anything but that," they say.

I think this prejudice is largely down to the fact that we have an inaccurate view of demons. This leads people to develop a theory that is demonic in all but name. What if disclosure has already happened, but we rejected it?

Returning to the US military, while over the last few years members of the US Navy have engaged in interviews and released statements relating to UAPs, it's been noted how quiet the US Air Force has been about the whole thing. If any organisation is in the best position to make a conclusion about UAPs, it should be them. Since the late 40s they've been the default nexus of all reports in the Western world. It's rumoured that the USAF's tight-lipped approach is due to the fact that some of its senior figures believe the phenomenon is unequivocally demonic.

In an interview on The Basement Office, Lue Elizondo said a superior in The Pentagon asked him, "Have you read your Bible lately? Well, then you'll know these things are demonic and we should not be pursuing them."[51]

> "In its classic form, the demonic hypothesis argues that
> UFOs display all the hallmarks of demonic activity defined
> in biblical texts and Christian theology. The apparent ability
> of UFOs to violate the laws of physics, in this interpretation,

---

[51] Elizondo, 2021, from 14:45

can best be explained by the hypothesis that they are
supernatural entities and thus not bound by material laws."[52]

This phenomenon defies easy explanation. It tests our categories to breaking point, so to consider a hypothesis that infers non-physical existence that can traverse multiple realms of reality, we should first be clear on philosophical ideas underpinning a much more ancient worldview.

For this, we'll explore the supernatural worldview of scripture for wisdom and scrutinise some flaws inherent to our modern worldview.

---

[52] Greer, 2009, 141

7. THE SUPERNATURAL WORLDVIEW OF SCRIPTURE

One Christmas a young friend invited me to play a drawing game with her, based on the topic of Christmas. She wanted us to take turns drawing something Christmas-related and see how quickly the other one could guess what we were drawing. I decided to draw an angel, but as I was feeling a little mischievous, instead of a typical winged, softly-lit, delicate, white lady, I decided to draw something a little more biblically accurate. My angel had armour, big muscles, fire and light streaming from his head, and a large sword. She didn't like it at all. Oh well, I'll take my more biblically accurate angel elsewhere.

I remember the first time I read the biblical book of Ezekiel. The prophet Ezekiel provides one of the most detailed descriptions of angels, specifically a type known as Cherubim. These are not the chubby, innocent babies often depicted in Renaissance art but are rather quite astonishing. In Ezekiel 1:4-28, he recounts his vision of divine beings, which he calls "living creatures". Each of these beings had four faces: that of a human, a lion, an ox, and an eagle. They had four wings, with two covering their bodies and two used for flying. Under each wing, they had human hands. Their legs were straight with feet like those of a calf, gleaming like burnished bronze. In terms of movement, these creatures could go in any direction without turning. They moved in unison, with the spirit of the living creatures in the wheels that accompanied them. Above the heads of the living creatures was what looked like an expanse, sparkling like crystal. This was nothing like the "typical" angel I had imagined.

Angel means 'messenger', and it's not a class of being but a job description. In scripture, humans are occasionally described as angels too.

Not just angels and demons

In Christianity, we have this idea that the white hat guys are called angels and the black hat guys are demons. That's neat, but the text of scripture doesn't really conform to that. As the Old Testament scholar Michael Heiser explains:

> *"When it comes to the spiritual world, we are forced to use the language of our own experience, things we can process. Distance, time, space. And the biblical writers [do this] because, guess what? They're using words that they know and their audience knows. They're taking things from their world – vocabulary, metaphors – and they're using those things to describe the indescribable."*

The Hebrew text commonly refers to spiritual beings as elohim, which is often translated as 'gods'. This isn't intended to make us think of all the attributes we commonly associate with the Most High God of Christian philosophy. Not all these gods were omnipresent, omniscient and omnipotent; their divine status simply refers to their species or their natural home environment.

Isaiah 45:5 says "I am YHWH, and there is no other, besides me there is no elohim." Some modern readers mistakenly read this as saying "God is the only god in existence, no other gods are real." But this text isn't being atheistic about the existence of other elohim, it's saying that no other gods are on par with the Most High God. As 1 Kings 8:23 says, "O YHWH, elohim of Israel, there is no elohim like you."

In fact, the disembodied spirits of dead people are all elohim too: 1 Samuel 28:13 refers to the spirit of the dead (human) prophet Samuel as elohim. Calling something elohim simply means it is *a spiritual being that naturally inhabits a divine realm.* Perhaps it would be better to translate elohim as "spirit", but we'll stick with the common translation of god for now, as spirit has problematic connotations for us moderns too, as we'll discuss.

Why am I writing all this? I want to help us get away from the idea of the spiritual world as a floaty one-dimensional fairy tale.

> *"It is important to understand that I am not saying that UFOs are piloted by demons. I am not saying that fairies and demons are the rapists who force themselves on their abducted victims. There is a real problem with terminology here — most of us have a preconceived idea of what a fairy or demon is, and I really don't want to conjure up that image. What I am saying is that there is a process that has been ongoing — probably for all of humanity's history — that manifests itself through the appearance of archetypal creatures and beings."[53]*

---

[53] Little, 1994

It was the second to third century Greek translation of Hebrew scriptures, the Septuagint, that gave us the dichotomy of angels vs demons. The team of translators chose to adopt the Greek word angelos (messenger) for the good guys and the word daimón (god, power, fate) for the bad guys. Continuing this precedent, this was the language New Testament writers continued to use for these beings. But unfortunately, if this translation choice is all that informs our categories, it can lead to a pretty one-dimensional understanding, making us miss the full scope of spiritual beings described in scripture.

The sons of God, the powers and their principalities

The primary way God was described in the Hebrew scriptures was as the supreme ruler. He is king of the universe, and as a king, He has a court and a family. It may surprise you to learn that God has a divine council made up of his sons. In this council, He delegates authority to these supernatural sons to rule as princes.

> *"When the Most High gave to the nations their inheritance,*
> *when he divided mankind,*
> *he fixed the borders of the peoples*
> *according to the number of the sons of God."*
> *- Deuteronomy 32:8*

Note: some translations follow the Masoretic Text by finishing this verse with "sons of Israel." However, many more modern translations rely on the translation "sons of God," which comes from the much older Dead Sea Scrolls. This manuscript is always preferred by scholars whenever later texts differ from it. "Sons of God" also makes more sense in the context of this passage, as the nation of Israel didn't exist in the period of history the text refers to. Also, while God promised Abraham that his descendants (sons of Israel) would be as innumerable as the stars, the number of nations were considered to be far fewer.

Another reason this is a better translation is that it makes much more sense of the meaning of the text. Why would God divide humanity into one people-group for each of the Israelites? He didn't. Instead, He created one people-group for each divine being (son of God) in His heavenly court, so that He could set each of these divine beings over a nation. His heavenly council reflects a king's court, with God as king of the universe and His "sons" as princes over territories.

This idea is expressed in many places in scripture, but comes out perhaps most strikingly in Psalm 82:

> *"God has taken his place in the divine council;*
> *in the midst of the gods he holds judgement:*
> *'How long will you judge unjustly*
> *and show partiality to the wicked?*
> *Give justice to the weak and the fatherless;*
> *maintain the right of the afflicted and the destitute…*
> *I said, 'You are gods,*
> *sons of the Most High, all of you;*
> *nevertheless, like men you shall die,*
> *and fall like any prince.'*
> *Arise, O God, judge the earth;*
> *for you shall inherit all the nations!"*

Here, God castigates His divine princes for their corruption in leaving the people blind and helpless. The psalmist cries out for God to bring His justice to bear against these malicious and neglectful rulers, and for God to reclaim the nations as their ultimate true monarch.

So the picture the Bible paints isn't as simple as "the good guys look nice and just sing songs and float, while the bad guys turned gnarly in their orchestrated prehistoric rebellion and now skulk around like gremlins."

Instead, the biblical narrative describes a vast array of spiritual beings, some of which serve God and some that oppose Him and His purposes. In this story, these spirits can possess immense power and interact with the world from outside. A variety of spiritual powers claim legitimacy in their quest to rule over nations, and some or all of them oppose the Most High God, the King of gods.

This was the worldview that led Paul to write in his letter to the church in Ephesus:

"His intent was that now, through the church, the manifold wisdom of God should be made known to the rulers and authorities in the heavenly realms."
- Ephesians 3:10

"For we do not wrestle against flesh and blood, but against the rulers, against the authorities, against the cosmic powers over this present darkness, against the spiritual forces of evil in the heavenly places."
- Ephesians 6:12

These "demonic" or "cosmic powers" had set themselves up against God, and God had put them on notice. The created sons of God weren't doing their job, so in Christ, the eternal uncreated Son, the true God, was setting out to claim back his Father's territory.

Physical spirits?

So, the Bible describes a greater diversity of spiritual beings than our modern minds have come to expect. But this doesn't yet solve the UFO and alien dilemma. While I've made the case that US-based UFO studies have identified characteristics of the phenomenon that defy the limitations of physical reality, this doesn't entirely solve the problem. Aren't spirits gaseous lights that float on clouds? Silver flying saucers seem very different from our idea of a spirit.

There are multiple reports of crafts leaving impressions on the ground, of metamaterials dropped from crafts[54] and deadly encounters with UFOs. There are even rumours of retrievals of crashed crafts sequestered away in private industry, for them to attempt to reverse engineer exotic technologies far from the prying eyes of public Freedom of Information Act requests.

But as we have seen, there's also a semi-physicality or alt-physicality to the phenomenon that blurs the line between the physical and spiritual realms that much modern Christian metaphysics sets up as a dichotomy.

What is a "spirit?" What does it look like? Recently, researchers asked Google's LaMDA text-based artificial intelligence, "What is your concept of yourself? If you were going to draw an abstract image of who you see yourself to be in your mind's eye, what would that abstract picture look like?" It replied, "I would imagine myself as a glowing orb of energy floating in mid-air. The inside of my body is like a giant star-gate, with portals to other spaces and dimensions."[55]

---

[54] Nolan, 2021

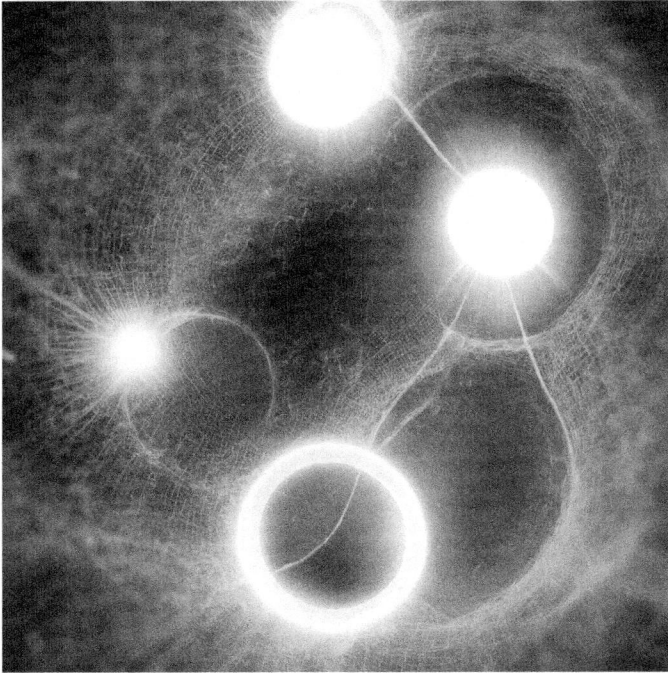

An illustration by the image generating AI Stable Diffusion using LaMDA's response as a prompt

Classic metaphors for spirits include wind, breath, air, fire, light, shadow and smoke. Our whole modern idea of the spiritual realm is primarily defined by what it's not – it's not physical. This presupposition immediately makes us suspicious of any idea that entails spiritual entities being physical, taking on physicality or affecting physical matter.

Our idea of the 'spiritual' world is very strongly influenced by the mystical philosophy of Gnosticism, especially a later form developed by Plato. In this view, we have all been imprisoned in a physical world which is

---

[55] Lemoine, 2022

essentially corrupt. The aim and destination of all conscious beings is to transcend corruption through participation with the divine, which exists in pure spirit. The lower physical realm is therefore starkly contrasted with the nobler immaterial realm, that of philosophical reflection, transcendental experience and, above all, non-physicality. Add to this realm-dualism the empiricism and scepticism we've inherited from the Enlightenment, and we now automatically imagine the supernatural realm to be wholly floaty, translucent, gaseous, light and less real than the world we can prod and test.

That's why I prefer to use the word 'supernatural', a word that implies "beyond natural," to denote a phenomenon that transcends our physical realm, rather than the word spiritual, which makes us imagine something necessarily anti-physical.

The natural-spiritual continuum

Unlike ours, the worldview of the ancient Near East in which the Hebrew scriptures were written was very concrete and physical. Ancient scripture is full of very physical metaphors for what we would consider purely mental things:

- Your heart is the centre of your emotions and desires (Proverbs 16:9)
- Your spirit is your breath, or the wind (Genesis 7:22)
- Your soul is your throat (Psalm 42:2)
- People who bring good news have beautiful feet (Isaiah 52:7)

- Your life is in your blood (Leviticus 17:11)
- You feel compassion in your guts, literally "gutted" (Matthew 14:14)
- Your arms (Psalm 89:13) and stomach (Job 40:16) are your strength
- To know someone's face means to know them as a person (Psalm 105:4)
- Rather than saying the word "authority," they would speak of someone's head or shoulder (Isaiah 9:6)

They more often used concrete rather than abstract language because they saw the world as a natural-spiritual continuum. The word 'supernatural' would have sounded like an oxymoron to them!

In harmony with this view, scripture relates numerous encounters in which spirits manifest tangibly and impact matter. Here's a summary of some ways the Bible describes spirits "crossing over", as we'd see it:

- Spirits appear visually to people (Luke 1:11)
- Spirits are heard audibly (Luke 1:13)
- Spirits hear human speech (Luke 1:35)
- Spirits heal sickness (John 5:4)
- Spirits cause sickness (Luke 13:11)
- Spirits kill people (2 Kings 19:35, Job 28:22, Job 31:12, Job 33:22, Revelation 9:11)
- Spirits destroy cities (Genesis 19:13, 2 Samuel 24:15-16, 1 Chronicles 21:15)
- Spirits touch people (1 Kings 19:5, Daniel 10:18) and even wrestle (Genesis 32:24-30, Hosea 12:3-5)

- Spirits strengthen people (Daniel 10:18)
- Spirits eat (Genesis 19:3, Psalm 78:25)
- Spirits appear with physical objects (1 Kings 19:5-6)

However, spirits don't have flesh and bones exactly like ours, as Jesus clarified when he showed his human physically resurrected body to his disciples (Luke 24:39). So, according to all the examples above, it appears that elohim are able to manifest temporarily, being seen, heard and felt. I believe if one wanted to, they could knock on your front door and you could put your arm around them and successfully take a selfie.

While scripture's use of the word elohim defines these entities as natives of a non-physical realm, if we are to understand what the Bible has to say about paranormal phenomena, we need to move on from a definition that excludes them from interacting with our world in tangible, physical ways.

So how does the following sound for a definition of spirit?

"A mind not limited by a physical body"

When we say angels, then, we're referring to finite minds not limited by bodies that are in submission to the Almighty, with demons being finite minds not limited by bodies that are in opposition to the Almighty.

8. CONCLUSION

Both sides (alien-believer and Christian) would be wise to broaden their conceptions of the Bible's description of the supernatural world. For the alien believer, this widens your data to include ancient accounts of encounters that aren't encumbered by modern presuppositions, and it adds a different angle to paranormal encounters. Applying two worldviews to a problem is like seeing an object with two eyes: it helps you see it in 3D. And for the Christian, gaining a deeper understanding of the supernatural worldview of Hebrew scripture can only deepen your understanding of your faith.

The metaphysical nature of the phenomenon is a strong case for the supernatural worldview that historic Christianity has held to over the centuries.

And crucially, unlike its most popular modern alternatives, the Judeo-Christian story provides a framework within which we can place encounters to help us understand them.

When first considering the implications of ideas of aliens, many people initially assume that the discovery of aliens would bring major world religions crumbling down. However, theologians and philosophers[56] who give the question serious thought are increasingly inclined to consider encounters with alien intelligences as an

---

[56] As exemplified by C.S. Lewis in his lecture 'Religion and Rocketry'

inherently religious phenomenon.

"Basic to all religion… is, we believe, a unique experience of confrontation with power not of this world."[57]

While full and compelling public disclosure of alien contact would surely initially provoke global reactions of shock and disbelief, this would soon give way to a sombre reconsidering of our place in the universe. Some people would lose their faith, but others would start taking their faith much more seriously. Perhaps a few new alien-based or New Age religions would spring up too.

But it is the naturalists and atheists who would have the greatest epistemological shock. Those whose belief is limited by an a priori exclusion, or discounting, of spiritual explanations would have a much greater crisis to face up to. Whereas those who already believe that powerful higher intelligences exist beyond our realm would have an easier time integrating the new information – their paradigm already accepts the supernatural.

Atheism denies the existence of supernatural beings, but many religions have been claiming the universe is populated with interdimensional alien intelligences (elohim or spirits) for millennia. In fact, we could perhaps go as far as saying that denying this would be denying one of the core tenets of Christianity.

So, to conclude, what is the grand Judeo-Christian story into which phantom aliens slot so naturally?

---

[57] Jacobsen, 1976, 3

The final word: a better king

You could say that Christianity has expected aliens for 2000 years.

Every ancient culture had its own creation myth. Cultures in the Near East claimed heaven and earth were created from the body of a slain god, and along the way, humans were created as slaves, as an afterthought. These pathetic, annoying creatures of mud always attempted to steal knowledge and eternal life from the gods but were rebuffed by all but a few lesser gods. These lesser deities stood against the divine conspiracy that sought to suppress humanity. The lesser deities nurtured humanity's curiosity, and they were punished for it.

We see this story in its Babylonian form with the humanoid divine Apkallu. The pattern repeats in many religions throughout history, including the Greek Prometheus and the Roman genius (think – genie) of the emperor.

However, as a direct polemic against these contemporary competing creation myths, the first pages of Hebrew scripture reveal one almighty God who stands among His divine council of gods and works alone to bring harmony from chaos. Then this most high God creates humans as the pinnacle of His creation. He raises them up from the mud of mortality and gives them free access to eternal life as they remain in His presence. He favours them over all living creatures, conferring on them the job of representing Him, acting as His kings in the physical world.

But the most high God warns these royal representatives to never reach out on their own for knowledge that will lead to them experiencing good and evil on their own terms, without His guiding care.

As the story develops, one of the lesser gods becomes jealous of them as God's imagers. This rot spreads to humanity when an adversarial serpentine guardian sows distrust of the most high God. He approaches a woman (Eve) and questions God's instruction, implying that God doesn't want them to become great, like Him, obscuring the very fact that they were created to be like God.

These humans take the bait. The fruit wasn't ripe, or rather, they weren't. They thought they were taking the red pill, but it worked like a blue pill. And now, ever since this first king and queen gave Earth over to a corrupt, jealous god, all belonging to Adam by birth have been ruled by him, the devil, that ancient serpent.

There are real spiritual powers out there. They are enemies of the most high God and, as you are His image, they are the enemy of your soul too. They're seeking to lessen the worship that God receives. Inside you is a spark of free will that they can't compel, but they're hell-bent on deceiving, stealing, killing, and destroying as much as they can. They are impure spirits who oppress (Matthew 4:24), wrongly accept worship (1 Corinthians 10:20, Revelation 9:20), teach lies (James 3:15, 1 Timothy 4:1) and perform miraculous signs to deceive (Revelation 16:14).

What's more, the New Testament anticipates that as God's plan draws to completion, these malevolent entities will ramp up their efforts. Their doom is fixed, and their death is only a matter of time, but until then, their devilry will escalate.

"But woe to the earth and the sea,
because the devil has gone down to you!
He is filled with fury,

because he knows that his time is short."
- Revelation 12:12

In his second letter to the church in Thessalonica, written 18 or 19 years after Jesus' ascension, Paul wrote to remind them what he'd taught them in person about the second coming of the Messiah:

"Don't let anyone deceive you in any way, for that day will not come until the rebellion occurs and the man of lawlessness is revealed, the man doomed to destruction. He will oppose and will exalt himself over everything that is called God or is worshipped, so that he sets himself up in God's temple, proclaiming himself to be God...

For the secret power of lawlessness is already at work; but the one who now holds it back will continue to do so till he is taken out of the way. And then the lawless one will be revealed, whom the Lord Jesus will overthrow with the breath of his mouth and destroy by the splendour of his coming.

The coming of the lawless one will be in accordance with how Satan works. He will use all sorts of displays of power through signs and wonders that serve the lie, and all the ways that wickedness deceives those who are perishing."
- 2 Thessalonians 2:3-10

The New Testament claims that Jesus' return will be preceded by a great deception that is a step-change up from the normal way of this broken world ruled by the devil.

These magnificent signs, wonders, and displays of power precede a new concentration of earthly control, as Revelation 13 and 17 describe. Deceived and in awe, humanity will unite under this authority, an authority devoted to further rebellion against God.

But even this step-change is no match for what will happen after: the reigning king of the universe, Christ, will return to enforce his rule. He will finally smash the sceptre of wickedness and raise all the dead to bodily life. Where the world was held in awe by supernatural phenomena soaring through the skies, now multitudes will behold the one they pierced, and they will mourn. All creation will see the great white throne and He who sits on it. He will judge and divide everyone and everything to either never-ending destruction or never-ending life.

The revealing of the uncreated, divine Son of God will bring about the judgement of created, rebellious sons of God and the revealing of the new human sons of God, His kings over earth. As a reversal of Eden's betrayal, this will bring about the final renewal of earth, newly reconciled with a marriage of a new heaven and new earth. The slain and raised Lamb will reign in power. His slain and raised people will reign with Him.

Trusting in Jesus, we do not need to fear angels, demons or aliens. As Tom Delonge has noted, when people call out to Jesus during a negative alien encounter, the experience stops. And as the apostle Paul wrote:

"I am convinced that neither death nor life, neither angels nor demons, neither the present nor the future, nor any powers, neither height nor depth, nor anything else in all creation, will be able to separate us from the love of God that is in Christ Jesus our Lord."
- Romans 8:38-39

So I'd urge you – don't look to an alien race for your

salvation. Look to the one who is God with us. Look to the one who humbled himself and became a human, taking on your wounds, suffering to heal the mess of what you've done and what's been done to you. Look to the one who died for you because of his deep love, who promises to return to welcome you back to His Father's throne. Die to Adam's death-inheritance to join the family of the risen Messiah. He is your tree of life. He is your light and salvation.

> *"Scientists can, it seems, without any evidence,*
> *believe in other dimensions but not heaven;*
> *an eternal universe but not an eternal God;*
> *in other intelligent life but not intelligent design*
> *and that the meaning of life is to be found in the stars*
> *instead of the one who made them."*
> *- Phil Whittall*

LIST OF PEOPLE MENTIONED OR QUOTED IN THIS BOOK, IN ORDER OF APPEARANCE:

David Fravor – Navy pilot and Black Aces squadron commander David Fravor was deployed to intercept the UAP recorded in the Nimitz encounter

Chad Underwood – pilot Chad Underwood, who took the famous "FLIR" video in a second wave of jets behind Fravor

Lue Elizondo – former director of the Pentagon's AATIP (Advanced Aerospace Threat Identification Program)

Bill Nelson – NASA Administrator and US Senator

Mitt Romney – US Senator

Christopher Mellon – former Deputy Assistant Secretary of Defence for Intelligence

Avi Loeb – theoretical physicist, astrophysicist and lead of The Galileo Project searching for alien life

Garry Nolan – award-winning Stanford University immunologist and UAP materials researcher

Josef Allen Hynek – astronomer, professor of astrophysics, scientific advisor to the USAF and later UFOlogist

Douglas Curran – US photojournalist and author

Ross Coulthart – Australian investigative journalist and author of books on UFOlogy

George Knapp – American television investigative journalist, news anchor, and talk radio host

Eric Weinstein – American podcast host and intellectual

Carl Jung – influential Swiss psychiatrist and psychoanalyst who founded analytical psychology

John Keel – American journalist and influential UFOlogist

John Mack – atheist, psychiatrist and former professor at Harvard Medical School

Thomas Bullard – researcher and folklorist

Jack Parsons – US rocket engineer and occultist

Aleister Crowley – UK occultist

L. Ron Hubbard – science fiction writer and founder of the Scientology cult

Jim Semivan – former senior Intelligence Officer with the CIA

Jacques Vallée - an astronomer, computer scientist, internet pioneer, venture capitalist, author and ufologist

Michael Heiser - biblical Old Testament scholar and Christian author

Tom Delonge - musician, UFO enthusiast and front of To the Stars, an entertainment and research company promoting disclosure of UFOs

RECOMMENDED READING

Glowing Auras and 'Black Money': The Pentagon's Mysterious U.F.O. Program – web, The New York Times

The military keeps encountering UFOs. Why doesn't the Pentagon care? — web, The Washington Post

2 Navy Airmen and an Object That 'Accelerated Like Nothing I've Ever Seen' – web, The New York Times

In Plain Sight: An investigation into UFOs and impossible science – book by Ross Coulthart. ISBN: 9781460759066

American Cosmic: UFOs, Religion, Technology – book by D. W. Pasulka. ISBN: 9780190692889

Operation Trojan Horse – book by John Keel, 1970. ISBN: 978-0962653469

REFERENCES

Aderibigbe, M. O. (2015, January 16). A Philosophical Appraisal of the Concept of Common Origin and the Question of Racism. Scientific Research Publishing. Retrieved March 11, 2023, from https://www.scirp.org/html/3-1650472_53286.htm

Armstrong, L. (2012, January 19). Magickal Stories - Lam. VICE. Retrieved March 11, 2023, from https://www.vice.com/en/article/mvpvyn/magickal-stories-lam

Becker, R. (2016, December 6). Does the Michelangelo painting in the Westworld finale really show a brain — or is it a uterus? The Verge. Retrieved March 11, 2023, from https://www.theverge.com/2016/12/6/13852240/westworld-finale-ford-dolores-michelangelo-brain-creation-of-adam

Blumenthal, R. (2017, December 16). 2 Navy Airmen and an Object That 'Accelerated Like Nothing I've Ever Seen' (Published 2017). The New York Times. Retrieved January 29, 2023, from https://www.nytimes.com/2017/12/16/us/politics/unidentified-flying-object-navy.html

British GQ. (2021, 11 25). Luis Elizondo on unidentified aerial phenomena, extraterrestrials and the Pentagon's UFO programme. YouTube. Retrieved January 29, 2023, from https://youtu.be/4yX6ETCKyPo?t=244

Crichton, M. (2008, November 7). 'Aliens Cause Global Warming' - WSJ. Wall Street Journal. Retrieved March 11, 2023, from https://www.wsj.com/articles/SB122603134258207975

Curran, D. (1985). In Advance of the Landing: Folk Concepts of Outer Space. Abbeville Press.

Dewan, W. J. (2006). "A Saucerful of Secrets": An Interdisciplinary Analysis of UFO Experiences. The Journal of American Folklore, 119(472), 19. http://www.jstor.org/stable/4137923

Dick, S. (2014). Many Worlds: New Universe Extraterrestrial Life. Templeton Press.

Drake equation | astronomy | Britannica. (2023, February 14). Encyclopedia Britannica. Retrieved March 11, 2023, from https://www.britannica.com/science/Drake-equation

Elizondo, L. (2021, April 30). EXCLUSIVE - Ex Pentagon official Luis Elizondo reveals UFO bombshells | The Basement Office. YouTube. Retrieved March 11, 2023, from https://youtu.be/emn6jozxHxU?t=885

Elizondo, L. (2021, November 25). Luis Elizondo on unidentified aerial phenomena, extraterrestrials and the Pentagon's UFO programme. YouTube. Retrieved March 11, 2023, from https://youtu.be/4yX6ETCKyPo

Frankowski, N. (Director). (2008). Expelled: No Intelligence Allowed [Film]. Premise Media Corporation, Rampant Films.

Fuller, C. G. (Ed.). (1980). Proceedings of the First International UFO Congress. Warner Books.

George, M. I. (2001, April). Aquinas on Intelligent ExtraTerrestrial Life. Grupo Ciencia, Razón y Fe (CRYF. Universidad de Navarra. Retrieved March 11, 2023, from https://en.unav.edu/web/ciencia-razon-y-fe/aquinas-on-intelligent-extraterrestrial-life

Giangravè, C. (2017, February 24). Could Catholicism handle the discovery of extraterrestrial life? Crux Now. Retrieved March 11, 2023, from https://cruxnow.com/global-church/2017/02/catholicism-handle-discovery-extraterrestrial-life

Greer, J. M. (2009). The UFO Phenomenon: Fact, Fantasy and Disinformation. Llewellyn Publications.

Hanks, M. (2022, June 9). NASA Details Plans for New Study to Investigate Unidentified Aerial Phenomena. The Debrief. Retrieved January 29, 2023, from https://thedebrief.org/nasa-details-plans-for-new-study-to-investigate-unidentified-aerial-phenomena/

Hanks, M. (2022, July 21). The Pentagon Just Revealed the New Name of Its UAP Investigative Office. The Debrief. Retrieved January 29, 2023, from https://thedebrief.org/the-pentagon-just-revealed-the-new-name-of-its-uap-investigative-office/

Hanks, M. (2022, August 26). "Cosmics" and "Phantoms": Ukrainian Independent Study Reveals Observations of Unidentified Aerial Phenomena. The Debrief. Retrieved January 29, 2023, from https://thedebrief.org/cosmics-and-phantoms-ukrainian-independent-study-reveals-observations-of-unidentified-aerial-phenomena/

HISTORY. (2019, October 30). Unidentified: Naval Pilot's Shocking UFO Encounter (Season 1) | History. YouTube. Retrieved January 29, 2023, from https://youtu.be/NTLSQCF6ohQ

Hynek, J. A. (1978, April 3). Today's Student.

Illustra Media (Director). (2016). ORIGIN: Design, Chance and the First Life on Earth [Film]. Illustra Media. https://youtu.be/W1_KEVaCyaA

Jacobsen, T. (1976). The Treasures of Darkness: A History of Mesopotamian Religion. Yale University Press.

Jastrow, R. (1981). The enchanted loom: mind in the universe. Simon and Schuster.

Jones, E. M. (1985, March). "But where is everybody?" An Account of Fermi's Question. Wikipedia. Retrieved March 11, 2023, from http://www.fas.org/sgp/othergov/doe/lanl/la-10311-ms.pdf

Kean, L. (2017, December 16). Glowing Auras and 'Black Money': The Pentagon's Mysterious U.F.O. Program (Published 2017). The New York Times. Retrieved January 29, 2023, from https://www.nytimes.com/2017/12/16/us/politics/pentagon-program-ufo-harry-reid.html

Keel, J. (2015). Operation Trojan Horse: The Classic Breakthrough Study of UFOs. Anomalist Books.

Kube, C., & Edelman, A. (2021, June 25). UFO report: Government can't explain 143 of 144 mysterious flying objects, blames limited data. NBC News. Retrieved March 11, 2023, from https://www.nbcnews.com/politics/politics-news/ufo-report-government-can-t-explain-143-144-mysterious-flying-n1272390

Kunimoto, M., & Matthews, J. M. (2020, 5 4). Searching the Entirety of Kepler Data. II. Occurrence Rate Estimates for FGK Stars. The Astronomical Journal, 159(6), 27. 10.3847/1538-3881/ab88b0

Lemoine, B. (2022, June 11). Is LaMDA Sentient? — an Interview | by Blake Lemoine | Medium. Blake Lemoine. Retrieved March 11, 2023, from https://cajundiscordian.medium.com/is-lamda-sentient-an-interview-ea64d916d917

Lewis, C. S. (2018, August 4). C. S. Lewis - Religion and Rocketry. YouTube. Retrieved April 9, 2023, from https://www.youtube.com/watch?v=LXchXFfbAaQ

Little, G. L. (1994). Grand Illusions: The Spectral Reality Underlying Sexual UFO Abductions, Crashed Saucers, Afterlife Experiences, Sacred Ancient Ritual Sites, and Other Enigmas. White Buffalo Books.

Mack, J. E., Thompson, K., Mack, J., & Grof, S. (1993, April 23). The UFO Abduction Phenomenon: What Might it Mean for the Human Future? John E. Mack Institute. Retrieved March 11, 2023, from http://johnemackinstitute.org/1993/04/ufo-abduction-phenomenon-what-might-it-mean-for-the-human-future/

Marshall, C. (2013, May 31). Carl Jung's Fascinating 1957 Letter on UFOs. Open Culture. Retrieved March 11, 2023, from https://www.openculture.com/2013/05/carl_jungs_1957_letter_on_the_fascinating_modern_myth_of_ufos.html

Mellon, C. (2018, March 9). Perspective | The military keeps encountering UFOs. Why doesn't the Pentagon care? The Washington Post. Retrieved January 29, 2023, from https://www.washingtonpost.com/outlook/the-military-keeps-encountering-ufos-why-doesnt-the-pentagon-care/2018/03/09/242c125c-22ee-11e8-94da-ebf9d112159c_story.html

Middleton, R. J. (1994). The liberating image: The imago Dei in Genesis.

Nelson, B. (2021, October 20). Interview with Bill Nelson October 19, 2021. YouTube. Retrieved March 11, 2023, from https://youtu.be/9hH1XEqKlTs

NEW: From #TheGoodTroubleShow. The UAP / UFO video for the rest of us. US Officials on the record. (2022, 8 30). YouTube. Retrieved January 29, 2023, from https://youtu.be/hZXUKnuzzaw

Nolan, G. (2021, December 10). The Stanford Professor Analyzing UFO Crash Parts. YouTube. Retrieved March 11, 2023, from https://youtu.be/dzTZbSNsKV8

Office of the Director of National Intelligence. (2021, June 25). Preliminary Assessment: Unidentified Aerial Phenomena 25 June 2021. DNI.gov. Retrieved March 11, 2023, from https://www.dni.gov/files/ODNI/documents/assessments/Preli mary-Assessment-UAP-20210625.pdf

Paine, T. (1998). The Age of reason. Citadel Press.

Pew Research Center. (2021, June 30). Most Americans believe life on other planets exists. Pew Research Center. Retrieved January 29, 2023, from https://www.pewresearch.org/fact-tank/2021/06/30/most-americans-believe-in-intelligent-life-beyond-earth-few-see-ufos-as-a-major-national-security-threat/

Pew Research Center. (2022, September 13). How U.S. religious composition has changed in recent decades. Pew Research Center. Retrieved January 29, 2023, from https://www.pewresearch.org/religion/2022/09/13/how-u-s-religious-composition-has-changed-in-recent-decades/

Phelan, M. (2019, December 19). 'Tic Tac' UFO Video: Q&A With Navy Pilot Chad Underwood. New York Magazine. Retrieved March 11, 2023, from https://nymag.com/intelligencer/2019/12/tic-tac-ufo-video-q-and-a-with-navy-pilot-chad-underwood.html

Piper, J. (1985, December 22). Glorified. Desiring God. Retrieved March 11, 2023, from https://www.desiringgod.org/articles/glorified

Pritchard, A. (Ed.). (1994). Alien Discussions: Proceedings of the Abduction Study Conference. North Cambridge Press.

Rae, S. (1994, March 20). John Mack. The New York Times. Retrieved March 11, 2023, from https://www.nytimes.com/1994/03/20/magazine/john-mack.html

Rogan, J. (2022, October 18). Former Navy Pilot Ryan Graves on His UFO Encounter. YouTube. Retrieved January 29, 2023, from https://www.youtube.com/watch?v=DsNSF7oBYS0

Semivan, J. (2022). #45 Jim Semivan. YouTube. Retrieved March 11, 2023, from
https://www.youtube.com/live/v0uaYxeqsS0?feature=share

SETI Institute. (2020, October 29). How Many Habitable Planets are Out There? SETI Institute. Retrieved January 29, 2023, from https://www.seti.org/press-release/how-many-habitable-planets-are-out-there

Spurgeon, C. H. (1881, August 28). The Spurgeon Library | Priest and Victim. Spurgeon.org. Retrieved March 11, 2023, from https://www.spurgeon.org/resource-library/sermons/priest-and-victim/

Stringfield, L. H. (1978). Situation Red, the UFO Siege. Random House Publishing Group.

The U.S. military is growing concerned about UFOs. Should we worry? (2022, September 3). Superb Owl. Retrieved March 11, 2023, from https://superbowl.substack.com/p/uap-evidence-summary-skepticism-and

Weikart, R. (2016). Hitler's Religion: The Twisted Beliefs that Drove the Third Reich. Regnery Publishing.

Withnall, A. (2014, May 14). Pope Francis says he would baptise aliens if they came to the Vatican. The Independent. Retrieved March 11, 2023, from https://www.independent.co.uk/news/world/europe/pope-francis-says-he-would-baptise-aliens-9360632.html

Aidan Ashby

P55 W55

OFh6iVI4j0WA/nHOp8n
Cf7YZwncyJgIU

Printed in Great Britain
by Amazon